The Grill Bible

Smoker Cookbook 100 Juicy BBQ Recipes

By Silvio Santi

TABLE OF CONTENTS

Introduction to BBQ Recipes

Barbecue, a time-honored culinary tradition, transcends simple cooking to become an art form cherished worldwide. From the smoky backyards of America to the vibrant street markets of Asia, the aroma of barbecue brings people together, evoking a sense of community, celebration, and cultural pride. This collection of BBQ recipes, meticulously curated for enthusiasts and novices alike, celebrates the rich diversity and universal appeal of barbecuing.

The Origins of Barbecue

"barbecue" derives from the Caribbean word "barbacoa," which refers to slow-cooking meat over an open flame or in a pit. The technique spread across continents, evolving uniquely in various regions. In the United States, barbecue culture is deeply rooted in Southern traditions, with each state boasting its style, from the vinegar-based sauces of North Carolina to the sweet, tomato-based sauces of Kansas City. Meanwhile, in South America, countries like Argentina and Brazil celebrate "asado," a grilling method highlighting the meat's natural flavors.

The Art and Science of Barbecue

Barbecue is more than just a cooking method; it combines art and science. The critical elements of great barbecue include the choice of meat, the marinade or rub, the cooking technique, and the wood used for smoking. Each of these elements can dramatically influence the flavor and texture of the final dish. Understanding the science behind how heat and smoke interact with the meat helps achieve that perfect balance of smokiness, tenderness, and juiciness.

Essential BBQ Techniques

Smoking: This method involves cooking meat at low temperatures over a long period, allowing the smoke to infuse the meat with deep, rich flavors. Popular woods for smoking include hickory, mesquite, applewood, and cherrywood, each imparting a distinct flavor profile.

Grilling: A quicker method than smoking, grilling cooks meat at high temperatures, searing the outside while keeping the inside juicy. This technique is ideal for cuts like steaks, burgers, and sausages.

Braising: Braising is a culinary method that combines slow cooking and grilling by searing the meat and boiling it in a tasty sauce. More challenging portions of meat turn out to be soft and tasty thanks to this technique.

Global BBQ Inspirations

Globally popular, barbecue is a product of many cultures, each contributing exceptional tastes and preparation methods. Here are some global sources of inspiration:

American BBQ: Think pulled pork, brisket, and ribs, often accompanied by coleslaw, baked beans, and cornbread.

Korean BBQ: Marinated meats, such as bulgogi and galbi, are cooked at the table and served with various side dishes (banchan), making this restaurant renowned for its participatory eating experience.

South African Braai: A social event where meats such as boerewors (sausages) and sosaties (kebabs) are grilled over wood fires.

Japanese Yakitori: Skewered and grilled chicken, often seasoned with tare sauce or simply salted, offering a delicious and straightforward BBQ experience.

Health and Safety Tips

Barbecuing, while delicious, requires attention to health and safety:

Proper Meat Handling: Keep raw and cooked meats separate to avoid cross-contamination. Use separate utensils and cutting boards.

Cooking Temperatures: Ensure meats are cooked to safe internal temperatures to prevent foodborne illnesses. For example, poultry should reach 165°F (74°C), while beef and pork should reach at least 145°F (63°C).

Fire Safety: Keep a close watch on the grill or smoker, especially using charcoal or wood. Have a fire extinguisher or water source nearby in case of flare-ups.

Conclusion

Barbecue, in its myriad forms, celebrates flavor, culture, and community. Whether you're a seasoned pitmaster or a backyard grilling enthusiast, this collection of BBQ recipes is designed to inspire and guide you on a culinary journey. From classic American ribs to exotic international dishes, these recipes will help you master the art of barbecue, creating unforgettable meals and memories for family and friends.

Fire up the grill, embrace the smoke, and let the flavors of BBQ transport you around the globe and back again. Savor the voyage and the delectable treats it offers.

100 JUICY BBQ RECIPES

1. CLASSIC BARBECUE RIBS

INGREDIENTS:

- ❖ 2 racks of pork baby back ribs
- ❖ 1 cup BBQ sauce
- ❖ 1/4 cup brown sugar
- ❖ 2 tablespoons paprika
- ❖ 2 tablespoons garlic powder
- ❖ 2 tablespoons onion powder
- ❖ 1 tablespoon chili powder
- ❖ Salt and pepper to taste

INSTRUCTIONS:

1. Use indirect heat to preheat your grill to 225°F (107°C). Establish a two-zone fire if you're using a charcoal barbecue.
2. The membrane below the ribs should be removed. Sprinkle salt and pepper on the ribs' two sides.

3. To make the dry rub, mix the paprika, brown sugar, onion, garlic, and chili powders in a small bowl.
4. Apply a thick layer of the dry rub mixture to the ribs on both sides.
5. The ribs should be placed over indirect heat on the grill. Once the ribs are soft and the meat begins to separate from the bones, cover the pot and simmer for three to four hours.
6. For the last thirty minutes of cooking, bast the ribs with BBQ sauce every ten minutes, rotating them occasionally to ensure an even glaze.
7. Once done, take the ribs from the grill and give them time to settle before slicing.
8. With additional BBQ sauce on the side, serve hot.

NOTE:

➢ You can change the cooking time depending on the thickness of the ribs and the level of tenderness you choose. Use a meat thermometer to ensure thermometer to ensure the internal temperature reaches.
➢ You can add wood chunks or chips to the grill while cooking for an additional smoky taste.
➢ Feel free to use homemade or your favorite barbecue sauce for this recipe.

2. SMOKED BRISKET

INGREDIENTS:

- ❖ 1 whole beef brisket (about 10-12 pounds)
- ❖ 1/4 cup kosher salt
- ❖ 1/4 cup black pepper
- ❖ 1/4 cup paprika
- ❖ 1/4 cup brown sugar
- ❖ 2 tablespoons garlic powder
- ❖ 2 tablespoons onion powder
- ❖ 1 tablespoon cayenne pepper (optional)
- ❖ Wood chunks or chips (hickory, oak, or mesquite) soaked in water for 30 minutes

INSTRUCTIONS:

1. Ensure the brisket has only approximately 1/4 inch of fat left outside by trimming off any excess. On the fat cap, score in a crosshatch pattern.
2. The kosher salt, paprika, black pepper, brown sugar, onion, garlic, and cayenne pepper (if used) should all be combined in a bowl to produce the dry rub.

3. Evenly coat the surface once the brisket has been liberally rubbed with the dry rub mixture.Brisket should be refrigerated for at least four hours or overnight under plastic wrap.
4. Let the brisket come to room temperature while you prepare the smoker.
5. Add your chips or pieces after preheating your smoker to 225°F (107°C).
6. After the brisket is placed, fat side up, on the smoking grate, close the cover. For every pound of meat, smoke the brisket for about an hour or until the thickest part reaches an internal temperature of 195–205°F (90–96°C).
7. Once the brisket reaches your desired doneness, remove it from the barbecue and gently cover it with aluminum foil. Give it at least thirty minutes to rest so the juices can spread.
8. Gently unwrap the brisket and cut it into 1/4- to 1/2-inch-thick slices, cutting against the grain.
9. Serve hot, with your favorite barbecue sauce on the side.

NOTE:

➢ Cutting the brisket against its grain is essential to ensure tenderness.
➢ The thickness, size, and consistency of the temperature in your smoker can influence the length of time the brisket takes to cook.
➢ Use a meat thermometer to check the brisket's internal temperature during cooking.

➢ You can add wood chunks or chips to the smoker while cooking for a more robust smoke flavor.

3. GRILLED CHICKEN WINGS

INGREDIENTS:

- ❖ 2 lbs chicken wings
- ❖ 1/4 cup soy sauce
- ❖ 1/4 cup honey
- ❖ 2 tablespoons olive oil
- ❖ 2 cloves garlic, minced
- ❖ 1 teaspoon paprika
- ❖ 1/2 teaspoon black pepper
- ❖ 1/2 teaspoon salt
- ❖ Optional: chopped fresh cilantro for garnish

INSTRUCTIONS:

1. In a bowl, combine soy sauce, honey, olive oil, paprika, black pepper, and salt for the marinade.
2. The chicken wings can be put in a shallow dish or a sizable plastic bag that can be sealed. Pour the marinade over the wings to ensure they are evenly coated. Let it marinate for at least an hour, or better still, all night.
3. Set your grill's temperature to medium-high.

4. After marinating the chicken wings, please remove them and throw away any extra marinade.
5. After preheating the grill, place the wings on it and cook for 10 to 12 minutes on each side, or until they are crispy and cooked through and measure 165°F (74°C) inside.
6. Top the grilled wings with finely chopped fresh cilantro after transferring them to a serving plate.
7. Warm-up and pair it with your preferred dipping sauce.

NOTE:
➤ You can modify the marinade's honey and soy sauce proportions to suit your tastes.
➤ Before grilling, add more paprika or your preferred spice blend to the wings for more flavor.
➤ To ensure consistent grilling, turn the wings halfway through cooking.

4. PULLED PORK SANDWICHES

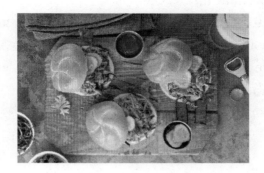

INGREDIENTS:

- ❖ 3 lbs pork shoulder or pork butt
- ❖ 1 onion, chopped
- ❖ 4 cloves garlic, minced
- ❖ 1 cup BBQ sauce
- ❖ 1/4 cup apple cider vinegar
- ❖ 2 tablespoons brown sugar
- ❖ 1 tablespoon Worcestershire sauce
- ❖ 1 teaspoon smoked paprika
- ❖ Salt and pepper to taste
- ❖ Hamburger buns or sandwich rolls
- ❖ Coleslaw (optional for serving)

INSTRUCTIONS:

1. Salt, pepper, and smoked paprika are used to season the pork shoulder or butt.
2. Add the chopped onion, minced garlic, brown sugar, apple cider vinegar, BBQ sauce, and Worcestershire sauce to a slow cooker.
3. After adding the sauce mixture to the slow cooker, place the seasoned pork shoulder or butt inside.
4. Once the pork is soft and quickly shreds with a fork, cook it covered over low heat for 8 to 10 hours.
5. Place
6. some coleslaw on top before covering it with the upper portion of the bun or roll.
7. Enjoy while hot!

NOTE:

➢ To change the pulled pork's flavor, add cayenne pepper, onion powder, garlic powder, or your favorite BBQ sauce. Pulled pork
➢ can be frozen for three months or refrigerated for three days in an airtight container.
➢ Pulled pork cooks faster in an Instant Pot or pressure cooker.

5. HONEY BBQ GLAZED SALMON

INGREDIENTS:

- ❖ 4 salmon fillets (about 6 oz each)
- ❖ 1/4 cup BBQ sauce
- ❖ 2 tablespoons honey
- ❖ 1 tablespoon soy sauce
- ❖ 1 tablespoon olive oil
- ❖ 2 cloves garlic, minced
- ❖ Salt and pepper to taste
- ❖ Chop fresh parsley or green onions for garnish.

INSTRUCTIONS:

1. Set your grill's temperature to medium-high.
2. To prepare the glaze, combine the olive oil, honey, soy sauce, BBQ sauce, minced garlic, salt, and pepper in a small bowl.
3. Arrange a comprehensive piece of aluminum foil over the salmon fillets. Generously brush the glaze over them, saving some for basting.
4. Put the salmon immediately on the grill grates within the foil. Once the salmon is cooked through and readily flakes with a fork, cover and simmer for another 8 to 10 minutes.

5. Use the remaining glaze to baste the salmon during the last few minutes of cooking.
6. When the salmon is cooked through, carefully take it off the grill and place it onto a dish.
7. Chop green onions or parsley to garnish.
8. Warm-up and pick teams.

NOTE:

➤ For this dish, you can use skin-on or skinless salmon fillets.
➤ When applying the glaze to skin-on salmon fillets, arrange them skin-side down on the foil.
➤ Make sure not to overcook the salmon to keep it juicy and tender.

6. BBQ BACON WRAPPED SHRIMP

INGREDIENTS:

- ❖ 24 large shrimp, peeled and deveined
- ❖ 12 slices bacon, cut in half crosswise
- ❖ 1/4 cup BBQ sauce
- ❖ 2 tablespoons honey
- ❖ 1 tablespoon soy sauce
- ❖ 1 tablespoon olive oil
- ❖ 1 teaspoon smoked paprika
- ❖ 1/2 teaspoon garlic powder
- ❖ Salt and pepper to taste
- ❖ Wooden toothpicks, soaked in water for 25-30 minutes

INSTRUCTIONS:

1. Set the heat on your grill to medium-high.
2. To prepare the glaze, mix BBQ sauce, honey, soy sauce, olive oil, garlic powder, smoked paprika, salt, and pepper in a small bowl.
3. Using a wooden toothpick, enclose each shrimp with a half-slice of bacon.
4. Distribute the glaze evenly over the shrimp wrapped in bacon.
5. Put the shrimp on the heated grill and cook for three to four minutes on each side until the shrimp turns pink and becomes opaque and the bacon is crispy.
6. Baste the shrimp with any residual glaze during the last few minutes of cooking.
7. When the shrimp are cooked through, carefully take them off the grill and place them onto a dish.
8. As a main course or appetizer, serve hot.

NOTE:

➢ To avoid burning them on the grill, soak the wooden toothpicks in water before using them.
➢ You can use any barbecue sauce in this recipe, depending on your tastes.
➢ Before grilling, add more smoked paprika to the shrimp for more flavor.

7. GRILLED VEGETABLE SKEWERS

INGREDIENTS:

- ❖ 2 zucchinis, sliced into rounds
- ❖ 2 yellow squash, sliced into rounds
- ❖ 1 red bell pepper, cut into chunks
- ❖ 1 yellow bell pepper, cut into chunks
- ❖ 1 red onion, cut into chunks
- ❖ 8 ounces mushrooms, whole or halved
- ❖ 1/4 cup olive oil
- ❖ 2 cloves garlic, minced
- ❖ 1 tablespoon balsamic vinegar
- ❖ 1 teaspoon dried oregano
- ❖ 1 teaspoon dried thyme
- ❖ Salt and pepper to taste
- ❖ Wooden skewers soaked in water for at least 25-30 minutes

INSTRUCTIONS:

1. Set your grill's temperature to medium-high.
2. Olive oil, minced garlic and balsamic vinegar, dried thyme and dried oregano, salt, pepper should all be combined in a big bowl and blended thoroughly.
3. Add sliced zucchini, yellow squash, bell peppers, red onion, and mushrooms to the marinade bowl. Toss until the veggies are covered uniformly.
4. Alternating between the various vegetables, thread the marinated veggies onto the moistened wooden skewers.
5. After preheating the grill, place the vegetable skewers on it and cook, flipping regularly, for 10 to 12 minutes or until the vegetables are soft and beginning to caramelize.
6. When the veggie skewers are done, remove them from the grill and place them on a serving dish.
7. Serve hot alongside rice, quinoa, or your preferred grain as an entrée or side dish.

NOTE:

➢ Change the vegetables in this recipe to suit your tastes or seasonal produce.
➢ Add herbs or seasonings to taste and marinate.
➢ Before grilling, immerse wooden skewers in water to avoid burning.

8. BBQ CHICKEN PIZZA

INGREDIENTS:

- ❖ 1 pizza dough (store-bought or homemade)
- ❖ 1/2 cup BBQ sauce
- ❖ 1 cup cooked chicken breast and shredded or diced
- ❖ 1/2 red onion, thinly sliced
- ❖ 1 cup shredded mozzarella cheese
- ❖ 1/4 cup chopped fresh cilantro
- ❖ Olive oil for brushing

INSTRUCTIONS:

1. Set your oven to max (260°C or 500°F).Heat pizza stones in the oven.
2. Flour a surface and roll out the pizza dough to the right thickness.
3. Roll the dough on parchment or a pizza peel.
4. Coat dough lightly with olive oil to prevent mushiness.
5. Evenly cover the greased dough with BBQ sauce, leaving a tiny border for the crust around the edges.
6. Over the BBQ sauce, distribute the cooked chicken breast and the sliced red onion.

7. Evenly distribute mozzarella cheese shreds on the pizza's top.
8. With caution, slide the completed pizza onto the hot pizza stone in the oven or straight onto a baking sheet if you're not using a stone.
9. A preheated oven should bake pizza for 10–12 minutes until the cheese is melted and bubbling and the dough is golden brown.
10. After baking, remove
11. the pizza and top it with fresh cilantro.
12. Let the pizza cool down for a few minutes before cutting and serving.

NOTE:

➢ You can alter this pizza by adding more toppings, like chopped jalapenos, sliced bell peppers, or crumbled cooked bacon.
➢ Thinner crusts require more dough and fewer toppings.
➢ You can bake the pizza dough for a few minutes before adding the toppings to get a crispier crust.
➢ You may use any BBQ sauce for this recipe, whether sour, spicy, sweet, or smokey.

9. BARBECUE TURKEY BURGERS

INGREDIENTS:

- ❖ 1 lb ground turkey
- ❖ 1/4 cup breadcrumbs
- ❖ 1/4 cup BBQ sauce
- ❖ 1/4 cup grated onion
- ❖ 1 clove garlic, minced
- ❖ 1 teaspoon smoked paprika
- ❖ 1/2 teaspoon ground cumin
- ❖ Salt and pepper to taste
- ❖ Hamburger buns
- ❖ Lettuce, tomato, red onion (optional, for topping)
- ❖ Additional BBQ sauce for serving

INSTRUCTIONS:

1. Set your grill's temperature to medium-high.
2. Combine ground turkey, breadcrumbs, BBQ sauce, smoked paprika, chopped garlic, shredded onion, ground cumin, salt, and pepper in a big bowl. Blend until thoroughly blended.

3. Make a patty from each of the four equal turkey mixture pieces.
4. Place turkey patties on a preheated grill. They should be 165°F (74°C) after 5–6 minutes on each side.
5. In the
6. last minute of cooking, add more BBQ sauce to the tops of the burgers.
7. Take the burgers off the grill when they're done, and let them rest for a while.
8. You can toast the hamburger buns over the fire if you want to.
9. Add lettuce, tomato, red onion, and extra BBQ sauce, if you like, to each bun, and then place a turkey patty on top of each one.
10. Enjoy while it's still hot!

NOTE:

➤ You can customize these turkey burgers by adding cheese, avocado, or fried bacon, among other things.
➤ Wait too long to cook the turkey burgers if you want them to stay juicy and tasty.
➤ You can use a plate or grill pan to cook these turkey burgers inside if you'd like to.

10. KANSAS CITY STYLE BURNT ENDS

INGREDIENTS:

- ❖ 3 lbs beef brisket point (also known as the deckle or fatty end of the brisket)
- ❖ 1/4 cup BBQ rub seasoning
- ❖ 1/4 cup BBQ sauce
- ❖ 2 tablespoons brown sugar
- ❖ 2 tablespoons apple cider vinegar
- ❖ 1 tablespoon Worcestershire sauce
- ❖ 1 tablespoon honey
- ❖ Salt and pepper to taste

INSTRUCTION:

1. Add your favorite wood chips or bits, such as hickory or oak, to get your smoker to 250°F (120°C).
2. Remove surplus fat from the brisket point's surface, preserving around 1/4 inch of fat.
3. Make careful to coat the brisket point uniformly on all sides by liberally applying BBQ rub flavor.
4. Close the smoker cover after setting the seasoned brisket point on the grate. Smoke until the internal temperature reaches approximately 165°F (74°C), which should take 4–5 hours.
5. Take the brisket point out of the grill and wrap it tightly in foil. Please put it back in the smoker and cook for another two to three hours until the meat is soft and juicy and the temperature hits about 200°F (93°C).
6. While the beef is cooking, make the glaze with the BBQ sauce. In a small pot, mix the honey, apple cider vinegar, brown sugar, Worcestershire sauce, and BBQ sauce. Over low heat, stir the sauce occasionally until it becomes a little thicker.
7. After the brisket is done, remove it from the smoker and give it a 15—to 20-minute rest.
8. Cut the brisket tip into 1-inch-long, bite-sized chunks.
9. After putting the brisket cubes in a big dish, toss them to coat them evenly with the BBQ sauce glaze.
10. Put the glazed brisket cubes back in the smoker and cook for thirty to sixty minutes or until the edges are crispy and caramelized.
11. Take the charred ends from the smoker and serve hot as a flavorful starter or entrée.

NOTE:

➢ For a delicious sandwich, you can serve the burnt ends on slider buns with pickles and onions or just as they are.

➢ For this recipe, use the point cut of the brisket as it has more fat and marbling, which contributes to the tender, juicy, burnt ends.

➢ You can modify the BBQ sauce and seasoning to suit your tastes.

11. TEXAS-STYLE BBQ BEEF RIBS

INGREDIENTS:

- ❖ 4 lbs beef back ribs
- ❖ 1/4 cup BBQ rub seasoning (store-bought or homemade)
- ❖ 1 cup beef broth
- ❖ 1/2 cup apple cider vinegar
- ❖ 1/4 cup Worcestershire sauce
- ❖ 1/4 cup yellow mustard
- ❖ 2 tablespoons brown sugar
- ❖ 2 tablespoons hot sauce (optional)
- ❖ Salt and pepper to taste
- ❖ BBQ sauce for serving

INSTRUCTION:

1. Texas flavor comes from preheating your smoker using oak or hickory wood to 225°F (107°C).
2. If needed, remove any extra fat from the beef ribs' surface.
3. Make careful to coat the ribs uniformly on all sides by liberally coating them with BBQ rub flavor.
4. To make the basting liquid, combine the beef broth, Worcestershire sauce, apple cider vinegar, yellow mustard, brown sugar, spicy sauce (if using), salt, and pepper in a small bowl.
5. After placing the spiced beef ribs, bone side down, on the smoker grate, cover it, and smoke it for three to four hours, or until the meat is fork-tender and separates from the bones.
6. To maintain the ribs' moisture and flavor, bast them once an hour using the basting liquid prepared.
7. After the ribs are cooked, remove them from the smoker and let them rest for ten to fifteen minutes before slicing.
8. For added taste, spray the ribs with BBQ sauce right before serving.
9. Serve the ribs hot, sliced between the bones, with your preferred BBQ sides.

NOTE:

➢ Since beef back ribs can be quite fatty, it's critical to cut any extra fat before smoking to avoid flare-ups.

➤ You can use any BBQ rub seasoning or combine spices like chili powder, paprika, garlic powder, onion powder, and cumin to create a blend.

➤ You can add wood chunks or chips to the smoker for a more pungent taste throughout the cooking process.

➤ To taste, adjust the amount of hot sauce in the basting liquid to suit your heat level.

12. BBQ PULLED CHICKEN SLIDERS

INGREDIENTS:

For the Pulled Chicken:

- ❖ 1.5 lbs boneless, skinless chicken breasts
- ❖ 1 cup BBQ sauce
- ❖ 1/4 cup chicken broth or water
- ❖ 2 tablespoons apple cider vinegar
- ❖ 1 tablespoon brown sugar
- ❖ 1 teaspoon smoked paprika
- ❖ 1 teaspoon garlic powder
- ❖ 1/2 teaspoon onion powder
- ❖ Salt and pepper to taste

For the Sliders:

- ❖ Slider buns
- ❖ Coleslaw (optional for topping)

❖ Pickles (optional for topping)

INSTRUCTION:

1. Texas flavor comes from preheating your smoker to 225°F (107°C) with oak or hickory wood.
2. If needed, remove any extra fat from the beef ribs' surface.
3. Make careful to coat the ribs uniformly on all sides by liberally coating them with BBQ rub flavor.
4. To make the basting liquid, combine the beef broth, Worcestershire sauce, apple cider vinegar, yellow mustard, brown sugar, spicy sauce (if using), salt, and pepper in a small bowl.
5. After placing the spiced beef ribs, bone side down, on the smoker grate, cover it, and smoke it for three to four hours, or until the meat is fork-tender and separates from the bones.
6. To maintain the ribs' moisture and flavor, bast them once an hour using the basting liquid prepared.
7. After the ribs are cooked, remove them from the smoker and let them rest for ten to fifteen minutes before slicing.
8. For added taste, spray the ribs with BBQ sauce right before serving.
9. Serve the ribs hot, sliced between the bones, with your preferred BBQ sides.

NOTE:

➢ Since beef back ribs can be quite fatty, it's critical to cut any extra fat before smoking to avoid flare-ups.

➢ You can use any BBQ rub seasoning or combine spices like chili powder, paprika, garlic powder, onion powder, and cumin to create a blend.

➢ You can add wood chunks or chips to the smoker for a more pungent taste throughout the cooking process.

➢ To taste, adjust the amount of hot sauce in the basting liquid to suit your heat level.

13. GRILLED CORN ON THE COB

INGREDIENTS:

- ❖ Four ears of corn, husks removed
- ❖ 2 tablespoons butter, softened
- ❖ Salt, pepper to taste
- ❖ Optional toppings: grated Parmesan cheese and chopped fresh herbs (such as parsley or cilantro), chili powder, lime wedges

INSTRUCTIONS:

1. Set your grill's temperature to medium-high.
2. Cover the corn ears equally by brushing them with softened butter.
3. To taste, salt and pepper to the corn to season it.
4. When the corn kernels are soft and slightly browned, place them directly on the grill grates and cook them for ten to fifteen minutes, rotating them occasionally.

5. When the corn is done, take it off the grill and place it onto a dish for serving.
6. Serve hot with your preferred garnishes, such as lime wedges, chili powder, chopped fresh herbs, or grated Parmesan cheese.

NOTE:

> If you like your corn to taste burnt, you can soak it in water for 15 to 30 minutes before grilling to prevent the husks from burning. However, this is not required.
> Feel free to experiment with different toppings and seasonings to suit your tastes.
> To conserve time and grill space, you can cook the corn with other items that you're grilling.
> You can remove the cob from leftover grilled corn and add it to soups, salads, or salsas.

INGREDIENTS:

For the Chicken:

- ❖ 4 boneless, skinless chicken breasts
- ❖ Salt and pepper to taste

For the Hawaiian BBQ Sauce:

- ❖ 1 cup BBQ sauce
- ❖ 1/4 cup pineapple juice
- ❖ 2 tablespoons soy sauce
- ❖ 2 tablespoons brown sugar
- ❖ 1 tablespoon rice vinegar
- ❖ 2 cloves garlic, minced
- ❖ 1 teaspoon grated fresh ginger
- ❖ 1/2 teaspoon onion powder
- ❖ 1/4 teaspoon ground cinnamon
- ❖ 1/4 teaspoon ground cloves
- ❖ Pineapple slices (for garnish, optional)

- ❖ Chopped green onions (for garnish, optional)

INSTRUCTIONS:

1. Heat your grill to medium-high.
2. Salt and pepper chicken breasts to taste.
3. In a small saucepan, mix BBQ sauce, pineapple juice, soy sauce, brown sugar, rice vinegar, minced garlic, grated ginger, onion powder, ground cloves, and cinnamon. After lowering heat from medium, simmer for 5–7 minutes, stirring occasionally, to thicken.
4. Grilling chicken breasts for 6–7 minutes
5. per side should reach 165°F (74°C).
6. Brush the chicken breasts generously with the Hawaiian BBQ sauce during the last five minutes of grilling, turning once to coat both sides.
7. When the chicken is cooked through, remove it from the grill and let it rest for a few minutes before serving.
8. Before serving, you can choose to top the grilled Hawaiian BBQ chicken with chopped green onions and pineapple slices.

NOTE:

> ➢ You can use skinless, boneless chicken thighs for the chicken breasts if preferred.
> ➢ You can experiment with the amount of rice vinegar and brown sugar to get the perfect balance of sweetness and tanginess for your BBQ sauce.
> ➢ For a full supper, serve the Hawaiian BBQ chicken over rice with a side order of grilled pineapple.
> ➢ Sliced leftover Hawaiian BBQ chicken is great for quesadillas, salads, wraps, and sandwiches.

15. BBQ PORK TENDERLOIN

INGREDIENTS:

For the Pork Tenderloin:

- ❖ 2 pork tenderloins (about 0.8 to 1.5 pounds each)
- ❖ Salt and pepper to taste

For the BBQ Sauce:

- ❖ 1 cup ketchup
- ❖ 1/4 cup apple cider vinegar
- ❖ 2 tablespoons Worcestershire sauce
- ❖ 2 tablespoons honey
- ❖ 1 tablespoon Dijon mustard
- ❖ 1 teaspoon smoked paprika
- ❖ 1 teaspoon garlic powder
- ❖ 1/2 teaspoon onion powder
- ❖ Salt and pepper to taste

INSTRUCTIONS:

1. Set your grill's temperature to medium-high.
2. On all sides, liberally season the pork tenderloins with salt and pepper.
3. The ingredients for the BBQ sauce—ketchup, apple cider vinegar, Worcestershire sauce, honey, Dijon mustard, smoked paprika, garlic powder, onion powder, salt, and pepper—should be combined in a small pot. Mix thoroughly to blend.
4. The sauce should be brought to a simmer over medium heat and simmered for five to seven minutes, stirring now and then, until it thickens a little. Remove it from the heat and place it aside.
5. Put the seasoned pork tenderloins onto the prepared grill. Using a meat thermometer, cook for 5 to 6 minutes on each side, rotating regularly, until the interior temperature reaches medium-rare 145°F (63°C) or medium 160°F (71°C).
6. During the final few minutes of grilling, brush the pork tenderloins liberally with the prepared BBQ sauce. Turn the pieces and continue brushing until the meat is equally coated and charred.
7. After the BBQ sauce has caramelized and the pork tenderloins are thoroughly cooked, remove them from the grill and let them rest for a few minutes before slicing.
8. Thickly slice the BBQ pork tenderloins and, if preferred, serve hot with additional BBQ sauce on the side.

NOTE

➢ To maintain the tenderness and moist texture of the pork tenderloins, avoid overcooking them.

➢ For added flavor, marinate the pork tenderloins in the BBQ sauce for a few hours before cooking.

➢ Slices of leftover barbecued pork tenderloin are excellent on salads, sandwiches, and wraps and when topped with mashed potatoes or rice.

16. BBQ MEATBALL SUBS

INGREDIENTS:

For the Meatballs:

- ❖ 1 lb ground beef
- ❖ 1/2 cup breadcrumbs
- ❖ 1/4 cup grated Parmesan cheese
- ❖ 1 egg
- ❖ 2 cloves garlic, minced
- ❖ 1 teaspoon dried oregano
- ❖ 1 teaspoon dried basil
- ❖ Salt and pepper to taste

For the BBQ Sauce:

- ❖ 1 cup BBQ sauce
- ❖ 2 tablespoons honey
- ❖ 1 tablespoon Worcestershire sauce
- ❖ 1 tablespoon apple cider vinegar
- ❖ 1/2 teaspoon smoked paprika

For the Subs:

- ❖ 4 sub rolls or hoagie buns
- ❖ 1 cup shredded mozzarella cheese
- ❖ Optional: Chopped fresh parsley (green onions for garnish)

INSTRUCTIONS:

1. Divide the BBQ meatballs a
2. mong the sub-buns. Top each meatball with shredded mozzarella cheese.
3. After the completed subs are placed on the baking pan, bake for five to seven more minutes or until the cheese is bubbling and melted.
4. Remove the BBQ meatball subs from the oven and, if you like, top them with finely chopped green onions or fresh parsley.
5. Enjoy while hot!

NOTE:

- ➢ For this dish, you may prepare your homemade BBQ sauce or store-bought BBQ sauce.
- ➢ Feel free to add more toppings to the subs, like pickles, bell peppers, or sliced onions.
- ➢ Leftover BBQ meatballs can be frozen for extended storage or kept in the refrigerator for up to three to four days in an airtight container.

17. SMOKED MAC AND CHEESE

INGREDIENT:

- ❖ Select pasta or elbow macaroni, 8 ounces
- ❖ 4 tablespoons butter
- ❖ 1/4 cup all-purpose flour
- ❖ 2 cups milk
- ❖ 2 cups shredded cheddar cheese
- ❖ 1 cup shredded mozzarella cheese
- ❖ 1/2 cup grated Parmesan cheese
- ❖ 1 teaspoon mustard powder
- ❖ 1/2 teaspoon smoked paprika
- ❖ Salt and pepper to taste
- ❖ Optional toppings: breadcrumbs, chopped crispy bacon, diced jalapenos

INSTRUCTION:

1. To smoke best, preheat your smoker to 225°F (107°C) and use your favorite wood chips or chunks. This recipe requires a pellet or smoker box.
2. Cook pasta or elbow macaroni per packaging instructions until al dente. Drain and set aside.

3. Butter in a large skillet or saucepan melts over medium heat. Make a roux by whisking flour for 1–2 minutes.
4. Carefully adding milk while whisking minimizes lumps. Stir the mixture constantly until thickened and boiling.
5. Add smoked paprika, mustard powder, grated Parmesan, shredded cheddar and mozzarella, salt, and pepper and reduce heat. Mix until cheeses melt and sauce is creamy.
6. Mix pasta or macaroni with cheese sauce after cooking.
7. Place mac and cheese in a big, ovenproof aluminum or cast-iron skillet for smoking.
8. Smoke the mac and cheese skillet for one to one and a half hours until the top is golden brown and the edges are boiling.
9. Sprinkle breadcrumbs, crispy bacon, or diced jalapenos on mac and cheese in the last 15–20 minutes of smoking for flavor and texture.
10. Remove smoked mac & cheese from smoker and cool before serving.
11. Serve hot as a delicious main or side.

NOTE:

➢ Adjust cheese types and quantities to personalize this dish. Provolone, Monterey Jack, and Gruyere
➢ are others.
➢ With 1/2 cup cream cheese or sour cream, cheese sauce may be creamier.

- Airtight containers can store leftover smoked mac and cheese for three to four days. Serve after oven or microwave reheating.

18. BBQ STUFFED BELL PEPPER

INGREDIENT:

- ❖ Halves and seeds removed from 4 big bell peppers of any color
- ❖ 1 lb ground beef or turkey
- ❖ 1 cup cooked rice
- ❖ 1 cup BBQ sauce, divided
- ❖ 1 small onion, finely chopped
- ❖ 2 cloves garlic, minced
- ❖ 1 cup shredded cheddar cheese
- ❖ Salt and pepper to taste
- ❖ Optional toppings: chopped fresh parsley, sliced green onions

INSTRUCTION:

1. Preheat oven to 375°F/190°C.
2. Coarsely grind turkey or minced meat and place over medium heat in a large pan.
3. Garnish the skillet with minced garlic and diced onion once the sirloin is done. After two to three minutes, the onion should become tender.
4. Combine the cooked rice and 1/2 cup of barbecue sauce with the meat in the skillet. Blend while stirring frequently over heat for two to three minutes. Season with salt and pepper.
5. Half of the shredded cheddar cheese should be melted into the filling while the skillet is removed from the heat.
6. The bell pepper slices should be arranged in a baking tray.
7. Pinch bell pepper halves together with the rice mixture and barbecue meat.
8. To complete the crammed bell pepper
9. s, utilize half a cup of barbecue sauce.
10. By roasting bell peppers
11. in foil for twenty-five to thirty minutes, they can become milder.
12. Once the foil has been removed, proceed to cover the packed bell peppers with the remaining half-cup of shredded cheddar cheese.
13. Simply reheat the baking dish for an additional five to ten minutes to allow the cheese to soften.
14. Serve the loaded bell peppers that have been baked for a few minutes.
15. Add the finely chopped green scallions or parsley.

NOTE:

➤ It is possible that maize, black beans, jalapeos, or diced tomatoescould be incorporated into the filling.

➤ Confirm whether bell peppers can be considered substantial.

➤ Bell peppers last three to four days in the fridge. Serve hot from the oven or microwave.

19. KOREAN BBQ SHORT RIBS (GALBI)

INGREDIENTS:

- ❖ 3 lbs beef short ribs, flanken cut (about 1/2 inch thick)
- ❖ 1/2 cup soy sauce
- ❖ 1/4 cup brown sugar
- ❖ 1/4 cup mirin (rice wine)
- ❖ 2 tablespoons sesame oil
- ❖ 4 cloves garlic, minced
- ❖ 1 tablespoon ginger, grated
- ❖ 1/2 onion, grated
- ❖ 2 green onions, chopped
- ❖ 1 Asian pear, grated (optional for sweetness)
- ❖ Sesame seeds, for garnish
- ❖ Sliced green onions for garnish

INSTRUCTIONS:

1. Combine soy sauce, brown sugar, mirin, sesame oil, shredded onion, grated ginger, minced garlic, and chopped green onions. Grated Asian pear is optional but adds a touch of sweetness.
2. The beef short ribs should be put in a shallow dish or a sizable plastic bag that can be sealed. Pour the marinade over the ribs to ensure they are well coated—Marinate in the fridge for at least two hours or overnight for optimal flavor.
3. Set your grill's temperature to medium-high.
4. Shake off any extra marinade before removing the short ribs from the marinade.
5. After grilling for two to three minutes on each side, the short ribs should be cooked to your preferred doneness and have excellent grill marks.
6. After the short ribs are done, move them to a serving plate.
7. Garnish with green onions and sesame seeds.
8. Serve the hot Korean BBQ short ribs over steamed rice with your preferred side dishes, including pickled veggies and kimchi.

NOTE:

➤ English-cut short ribs can be substituted for the usual flank-cut short ribs used in Korean barbecue, but the former is recommended.
➤ If you don't have a grill, you can cook the short ribs on a stovetop grill pan or broil them in the oven.

- For additional flavor, grill the ribs with leftover marinade.
- Adjust the marinade's sweetness and saltiness by adding soy sauce and brown sugar to taste.
- Use leftover marinade as a serving sauce
- by boiling it.
- Enjoy delicious Korean BBQ short ribs or galbi!

20. BBQ PULLED JACKFRUIT SANDWICHES

INGREDIENTS:

For the BBQ Pulled Jackfruit:

- ❖ two cans of young green jackfruit in water or brine, drained and rinsed
- ❖ 1 tablespoon olive oil
- ❖ 1/2 onion, finely chopped
- ❖ 2 cloves garlic, minced
- ❖ 1 cup BBQ sauce
- ❖ 1/2 cup vegetable broth or water
- ❖ 1 tablespoon maple syrup or brown sugar
- ❖ 1 tablespoon soy sauce or tamari
- ❖ 1 teaspoon smoked paprika
- ❖ 1/2 teaspoon chili powder
- ❖ Salt and pepper to taste

For the Sandwiches:

- ❖ Hamburger buns or sandwich rolls
- ❖ Coleslaw (optional for topping)
- ❖ Pickles (optional for topping)

INSTRUCTION:

1. In a big skillet, the olive oil is getting hot over medium heat. Cook minced garlic and onion for two or three minutes to soften and impart aroma.
2. Using a fork or spatula, crumble the washed and drained jackfruit into the skillet until it resembles pulled meat.
3. Add the smoked paprika, chili powder, maple syrup, brown sugar, tamari or soy sauce, BBQ sauce, and vegetable broth or water. Toss to blend well.
4. After lowering the heat to low, covering, and letting the jackfruit simmer for 20 to 25 minutes—while stirring now and then using a fork to crush any large pieces—until it becomes soft and absorbs the flavors of the sauce. If the mixture is too dry, add more water or vegetable broth.
5. Taste the soft jackfruit and add salt and pepper as needed.
6. If preferred, toast the sandwich rolls or hamburger buns.
7. Spoon the pulled jackfruit from the BBQ onto the bottom half of each bread to assemble the sandwiches. If desired, place pickles and coleslaw on top before covering with the upper portion of the sandwich.
8. Warm up the pulled jackfruit sandwiches with BBQ sauce and your preferred sides.

NOTE:

➤ Young green jackfruit, with its fibrous texture and neutral flavor, works well as a vegan alternative to pulled pork in this recipe.

➤ Sweetened jackfruit does not work well in savory recipes, so make sure you use canned jackfruit in water or brine rather than syrup.

➤ To suit your tastes, adjust the amount of seasoning and BBQ sauce.

➤ After three to four days, leftover BBQ-pulled jackfruit can be reheated and served in an airtight container in the refrigerator.

➤ Savor your tasty and filling pulled jackfruit sandwiches with BBQ sauce!

INGREDIENTS:

For the Dry Rub:

- ❖ 1/4 cup brown sugar
- ❖ 2 tablespoons paprika
- ❖ 1 tablespoon garlic powder
- ❖ 1 tablespoon onion powder
- ❖ 1 tablespoon chili powder
- ❖ 1 tablespoon ground black pepper
- ❖ 1 tablespoon ground cumin
- ❖ 1 tablespoon ground mustard
- ❖ 1 tablespoon salt
- ❖ 1 teaspoon cayenne pepper (adjust to taste for spiciness)
- ❖ Optional: 1 tsp dried thyme, oregano
- ❖ Two pork spare or baby back rib racks
- ❖ Optional yellow mustard binding

INSTRUCTION:

1. Use indirect heat to heat your smoker or grill to 225°F (107°C). Smoke your favorite apple, hickory, or oak wood.
2. Brown sugar, paprika, ground mustard, black pepper, cumin, garlic powder, onion powder, chili powder, salt, and cayenne pepper should be mixed in a small dish for the dry rub. Blend well until combined.
3. To let taste permeate the meat, remove the membrane from the back of the ribs.
4. Apply a little yellow mustard to both sides of the ribs. You can skip this, but it helps the dry rub stick to meat.
5. Apply a thick amount of dry rub mixture on both sides of the ribs, pressing it into the flesh to stick.
6. While you get the grill or smoker ready, let the ribs rest at room temperature for about 15 to 20 minutes. Let the flavors
7. fully immerse themselves in this way.
8. After placing the ribs meat-side down on the grill or smoker, close the cover. Cook for 3–4 hours, monitoring temperature periodically to maintain 225°F (107°C). Keep the smoke rolling with more wood bits or chunks.
9. Make sure the ribs are done after the first three to four hours. The meat and the bark should be soft and pleasant to the touch. To check the doneness of a rib bone, gently pull it away from the meat; it should come away with ease.
10. After cooking, remove the ribs from the grill or smoker and let them rest for five to ten minutes before slicing and serving.

11. Serve the hot, dry-rubbed Memphis-style ribs with your preferred side dish of barbecue sauce, coleslaw, baked beans, cornbread, or other traditional BBQ sides.

NOTE:

➢ You are welcome to modify the dry rub's cayenne pepper content to your desired degree of spice.

➢ Any excess dry rub can be preserved later in an airtight jar kept in an excellent, dry location.

➢ You can also cover the ribs with aluminum foil halfway through cooking to help keep moisture in and improve softness for even more flavor.

➢ Usually served dry to highlight the flavor of the dry rub, Memphis-style ribs can optionally be lightly coated with BBQ sauce in the last 15 to 30 minutes of cooking.

➢ The cooking time for spare ribs should be adjusted depending on the type of ribs you use, as they usually require a longer cooking time than baby back ribs.

➢ Savor your mouthwatering dry-rub ribs in the Memphis manner!

22. BOURBON GLAZED BBQ CHICKEN

INGREDIENTS:

For the Chicken:

- ❖ 4 bone-in, skin-on chicken thighs
- ❖ Salt and pepper to taste

For the Bourbon Glaze:

- ❖ 1/2 cup bourbon
- ❖ 1/2 cup ketchup
- ❖ 1/4 cup brown sugar
- ❖ 2 tablespoons apple cider vinegar
- ❖ 2 tablespoons Worcestershire sauce
- ❖ 2 cloves garlic, minced
- ❖ 1 teaspoon smoked paprika
- ❖ 1/2 teaspoon onion powder
- ❖ 1/4 teaspoon cayenne pepper (optional for heat)

INSTRUCTIONS:

1. Set your grill's temperature to medium-high.
2. On both sides, liberally season the chicken thighs with salt and pepper.
3. Bourbon, ketchup, brown sugar, apple cider vinegar, Worcestershire sauce, smoked paprika, onion powder, cayenne pepper (if using), salt and pepper should all be combined in a small saucepan. Mix thoroughly to blend.
4. Simmer the mixture over medium heat for 8–10 minutes, stirring occasionally, until the flavors meld and the glaze thickens. Stop cooking and set aside.
5. Grill skin-side-down seasoned chicken thighs. Bake the chicken for 5–6 minutes per side until the skin is grill-marked and the internal temperature is 165°F (74°C).
6. In the
7. final five minutes of cooking, heavily glaze the chicken thighs with bourbon, flipping once to coat both sides. Reserve glaze for serving.
8. When the chicken is cooked through, remove it from the grill and let it rest for a few minutes before serving.
9. Serve the hot, bourbon-glazed BBQ chicken thighs with your favorite barbecue sides and a dollop more whiskey glaze.

NOTE:

➤ If you prefer, you can use boneless or skinless chicken breasts or thighs instead of bone-in ones. Simply modify the cooking duration to guarantee they are well done.

➤ The chicken thighs can be marinated in bourbon for 30 to 1 hour before grilling, then patted dry and seasoned. This will result in a richer bourbon taste.

➤ You may easily change the amount of cayenne pepper in the glaze to your desired heat level.

➤ Leftover bourbon-glazed BBQ chicken can be kept in an airtight container for up to three to four days for up to three to four days and warmed up before serving.

➤ Savor this succulent BBQ chicken with a bourbon glaze!

23. GRILLED SHRIMP TACOS WITH MANGO SALSA

INGREDIENTS:

For the Grilled Shrimp:

- ❖ 1 lb large shrimp, peeled and deveined
- ❖ 2 tablespoons olive oil
- ❖ 2 cloves garlic, minced
- ❖ 1 teaspoon chili powder
- ❖ 1/2 teaspoon cumin
- ❖ Salt and pepper to taste
- ❖ 8 small corn or flour tortillas

For the Mango Salsa:

- ❖ 1 ripe mango, peeled and diced
- ❖ 1/2 red onion, finely chopped
- ❖ 1/2 red bell pepper, diced
- ❖ 1/4 cup fresh cilantro, chopped
- ❖ Juice of 1 lime
- ❖ Salt and pepper to taste

For Serving:

- ❖ Avocado slices
- ❖ Shredded lettuce or cabbage
- ❖ Sour cream or Greek yogurt
- ❖ Lime wedges

INSTRUCTIONS:

1. Mix olive oil, minced garlic, cumin, chili powder, salt, and pepper in a bowl. To equally coat peeled and deveined shrimp with marinade, toss them in the basin. Keep them marinating for 15–20 minutes while you grill and make mango salsa.
2. Heat your grill to medium-high.
3. In a separate bowl, mix mango, red onion, bell pepper and cilantro, lime juice, salt, and pepper. Set aside after combining well.
4. Thread marinated shrimp onto skewers or place them directly on barbecue grates. The shrimp should be pink and opaque after 2–3 minutes on each side of the grill.
5. While the shrimp browns, grill the tortillas for 30 seconds per side until tender and slightly browned. Keep them warm with foil or a clean kitchen towel.
6. Remove shrimp from grill and arrange on serving platter.
7. Top each warm tortilla with prawns to make tacos. Slice avocado, shred cabbage or lettuce, spoon mango salsa, and top with Greek yogurt or sour cream. Squeeze lime over top for flavor.
8. Quickly serve mango salsa and grilled shrimp tacos with extra lime wedges.

NOTE:

- ➢ Chopped tomatoes, sliced jalapenos, and crumbled cotija cheese are just a few of the topping options that go well with these tacos.
- ➢ You can still make do with a stovetop skillet or grill pan if you don't have a grill.
- ➢ The salsa and marinade can be adjusted to your liking by adjusting the amounts of chili powder and lime juice.
- ➢ If you make extra grilled shrimp tacos and put them in an airtight container, you can eat them within a day or two. Make the tacos ahead of time to keep the tortillas from getting soggy, but reheat the shrimp just before serving.
- ➢ Indulge in the flavors of your grilled shrimp tacos with mango salsa.

24. SMOKED PORK BELLY BURNT ENDS

INGREDIENTS

- ❖ Four to five pounds of pork belly
- ❖ a couple of tablespoons olive oil
- ❖ Mash ¼ cup of brown sugar.
- ❖ Two tablespoons of coarse Kosher salt (use the appropriate salt, please!)
- ❖ 1 Tablespoon freshly ground black pepper
- ❖ 1 Tablespoon paprika
- ❖ One teaspoon of chili powder
- ❖ ½ teaspoon garlic powder
- ❖ ½ teaspoon onion powder
- ❖ ¼ teaspoon cayenne pepper
- ❖ Sauce
- ❖ ½ to 1 cup BBQ sauce

- ❖ 4 Tablespoon salted butter
- ❖ ⅓ cup honey
- ❖ Cook Mode
- ❖ Prevent your screen from going dark

INSTRUCTIONS

1. Remove the pork belly's skin and the outermost layer of pure fat. The beef should be cut into ½-inch cubes.
2. Drizzle the meat with olive oil, then mix the rub ingredients and liberally sprinkle it on the meat, working it in to coat every piece.
3. After positioning the pork belly cubes on a wire cooling and baking rack, smoke them for two and a half to three hours at a temperature between 225°F and 250°F, or until they become a deep red color and a beautiful bark begins to form.
4. After transferring the pork belly cubes to a disposable aluminum pan, stir them to coat them equally with butter, honey, and BBQ sauce.
5. Cover and return the pork belly to the smoker for another 60 to 90 minutes to cook, or until a digital meat thermometer reads 200°F to 205°F when placed in the center of one of the burnt ends, or until a toothpick inserted into the ends easily comes out.
6. After removing the foil and cooking the pork belly burnt ends uncovered for fifteen minutes, remove them from the smoker and serve.

NOTES:

➤ The charred ends of pork belly are delicious when smoked with cherry wood. We haven't given any of these a go yet, but I've heard that hickory, pecan, maple, and fruit woods like apple and peach work well with pork like this.

➤ Storage: Leftover charred ends of pork belly should be kept in the refrigerator in an airtight container for three to four days. They reheat rather nicely in an oven set to 350 degrees Fahrenheit for fifteen minutes, or you can always put them back on the smoker.

25. BBQ PULLED PORK NACHOS

INGREDIENTS:

- ❖ 1 pound (about 450g) pulled pork (homemade or store-bought)
- ❖ 1 bag of tortilla chips
- ❖ 1 cup shredded cheddar cheese
- ❖ 1 cup shredded Monterey Jack cheese
- ❖ 1/2 cup BBQ sauce (plus extra for serving)
- ❖ 1/4 cup diced red onion
- ❖ 1/4 cup diced green bell pepper
- ❖ 1/4 cup diced tomato
- ❖ 1/4 cup sliced jalapeños (optional)
- ❖ 1/4 cup chopped fresh cilantro
- ❖ Sour cream, guacamole, and salsa for serving

INSTRUCTIONS:

1. Bring the Oven to 375°F, or 190°C, before you begin baking.

2. To make cleaning a snap, line a baking pan with parchment paper or aluminum foil.
3. The Pulled Pork Must Be Prepared: Follow the package directions to warm the store-bought pulled pork. Make sure the meat is cooked and shredded
4. before creating homemade pulled pork.
5. Put the Nachos Together: Evenly distribute the tortilla chips across the baking sheet that has been preheated. Distribute half of the shredded Monterey Jack and cheddar cheese over the snacks. Evenly distribute the pulled pork on top of the cheesy layer. Evenly coat the pulled pork with the BBQ sauce. Add the rest of the cheese.
6. Optional Add-Ons: Once the nachos are covered in cheese, top them with diced red onion, green bell pepper, tomato, and sliced jalapeños (if desired).
7. Cook: Melt and bubble the cheese in the oven for 10 to 12 minutes, or until the baking sheet is covered.
8. Before serving, take the nachos out of the oven and garnish with chopped cilantro. Garnish with extra salsa, guacamole, sour cream, and BBQ sauce before serving.

NOTE:

➢ Please feel free to adjust the toppings to your liking. Top with corn kernels, chopped olives, black beans, or whatever else your heart desires for nachos.
➢ To make the nachos even crispier, broil them for a minute or two after baking; just be careful not to let them burn.

➤ The cheese should be ooey and the toppings should be hot when you eat these nachos right out of the oven.

26. SMOKED BEEF BRISKET TACOS

INGREDIENTS:

- ❖ 2 lbs (about 900g) beef brisket, trimmed of excess fat
- ❖ Salt and black pepper to taste
- ❖ 2 tablespoons olive oil
- ❖ 1 onion, finely chopped
- ❖ 3 cloves garlic, minced
- ❖ 1 cup beef broth
- ❖ 1 cup salsa (your favorite variety)
- ❖ 2 teaspoons chili powder
- ❖ 1 teaspoon ground cumin
- ❖ 1 teaspoon smoked paprika
- ❖ 1/2 teaspoon dried oregano
- ❖ Corn or flour tortillas
- ❖ Toppings: diced onion, chopped cilantro, sliced jalapeños, lime wedges, shredded cheese, sour cream, salsa, avocado slices, etc.

INSTRUCTIONS:

1. Before cooking, liberally sprinkle salt and black pepper on both sides of the beef brisket.
2. Put the smoker on high heat (225°F, 107°C) and season it with hickory, mesquite, or oakchips or pieces if you want.
3. Brisket should be seasoned and covered before smoking. Place brisket on smoking grates after 1.5 to 2 hours per pound, or until internal temperature reaches 200°F (93°C). The normal cooking time is 8–10 hours, depending on the amount of brisket and smoking uniformity.
4. To make the braising liquid, heat up a big pan or Dutch oven and add the olive oil. After three to four minutes, when the garlic and onion have softened and released their perfume, add them to the pan.
5. To braise the brisket, add the beef stock and then the cumin, dried oregano, smoked paprika, chili powder, and salsa. Incorporate all components. Carefully add the smoked brisket to the braising liquid after placing it in the pan or Dutch oven. To make sure the beef is fork-tender and easily shreds, cook it gently covered for around 2-3 hours.
6. Once the brisket is cooked, take it out of the braising liquid and place it on a chopping board so it can be shredded. Use two forksto shred the meat.
7. Preheat the tortillas on a griddle or in a preheated oven for a few minutes before assembling the tacos. Before topping off your tacos, spoon a generous quantity of shredded brisket onto each tortilla. Add diced onion,

chopped cilantro, sliced jalapeños, and lime juice, if you want.

8. Warm the tacos on a dish and serve immediately, garnishing with additional toppings and sides as desired.

NOTE:

- ➤ To enhance the flavor, marinate the brisket the night before to smoking. A paste can be made by blending olive oil or mustard with spices such cayenne pepper, garlic powder, onion powder, and brown sugar.
- ➤ You are welcome to alter the taco toppings to suit your tastes. Delicious additions include avocado slices, chopped tomatoes, shredded lettuce, and a splash of spicy sauce.

27. BBQ CHICKEN QUESADILLAS

INGREDIENTS:

- ❖ 2 cups cooked chicken and shredded (you can use leftover grilled or roasted chicken)
- ❖ 1/2 cup BBQ sauce
- ❖ 4 large flour tortillas
- ❖ 2 cups shredded cheese (cheddar, Monterey Jack, or a blend)
- ❖ 1/2 red onion, thinly sliced
- ❖ 1/4 cup chopped fresh cilantro
- ❖ 1 jalapeño, thinly sliced (optional)
- ❖ Cooking spray or olive oil for cooking

INSTRUCTIONS:

1. Cook the BBQ Chicken: Place the shredded chicken in a bowl and toss to cover it entirely with BBQ sauce. Put aside.
2. To put the quesadillas together, Spoon two tortillas onto a sanitized surface. After dividing the shredded cheese equally

among them, spread it evenly over one half of each tortilla. Add the BBQ chicken mixture, sliced jalapeño (if using), chopped cilantro, and sliced red onion on top of the cheese.

3. To make a half-moon shape, fold the tortillas in half lengthwise over the filling. Then, cook. To seal, gently press down.
4. Get the quesadillas cooked: In a large griddle or skillet, mix the heat to medium. Sprinkle the surface with a little olive oil or cooking spray. Cook the quesadillas for two or three minutes per side, or until the tortillas are crispy and golden brown
5. , and the cheese has melted. Carefully transfer the prepared tortillas to the skillet.
6. After the quesadillas are cooked through, take them off the griddle and set them on a cutting board. Slice and serve. After the quesadillas have cooled for a minute, cut them into wedges with a sharp knife or pizza cutter.
7. Heat up some guacamole, salsa, sour cream, or BBQ sauce and serve the sliced BBQ chicken quesadillas on a platter.

NOTE:

➤ Feel free to add your preferred ingredients to the filling. You can add sautéed bell peppers, diced tomatoes, black beans, or corn kernels for additional taste and texture.
➤ If you like your barbecue sauce hotter, you can use a spicier BBQ sauce or increase the amount of chopped jalapeños in the filling.
➤ Before cooking, brush each quesadilla's outside with melted butter for a crispy finish.
➤ You can also cook these quesadillas on a grill or in a panini press for extra flavor.

28. GRILLED PORTOBELLO MUSHROOM BURGERS

INGREDIENTS:

- ❖ 4 large portobello mushroom caps
- ❖ 4 burger buns
- ❖ 4 slices of cheese (your choice, such as Swiss, cheddar, or provolone)
- ❖ 2 tablespoons olive oil
- ❖ 2 tablespoons balsamic vinegar
- ❖ 2 cloves garlic, minced
- ❖ Salt and black pepper to taste
- ❖ Burger toppings: lettuce, tomato slices, red onion slices, avocado slices, mayo, mustard, ketchup, etc.

INSTRUCTIONS:

1. To make the marinade, whisk together the olive oil, balsamic vinegar, salt, black pepper, and minced garlic in a small bowl.

2. Let the mushrooms marinate. Clean the portobello mushroom caps and pick the stems off. Put the mushrooms in a plastic bag that can be sealed or on a shallow plate. Pour the marinade over the mushrooms to make sure they are thoroughly coated. To guarantee even marinating, let the mushrooms sit in the refrigerator for at least 30 minutes and as long as 2 hours, flipping them over from time to time.

3. Before using the grill, preheat it to a medium-high temperature (between 375 and 400°F, or 190 and 200°C). To avoid sticking, make sure the grates are spotless and lightly oiled.

4. Grill the Mushrooms: While the grill is heating up, take the marinated mushrooms out of the refrigerator and allow them to come to room temperature. With the gills facing down, place the mushrooms on the heated grill. Grill the mushrooms on each side for 4–5 minutes until they are soft and marked with grill marks.

5. Cheese Addition (Optional): In the final minute of grilling, cover each mushroom with a melted slice of cheese.

6. Toast the Burger Buns: Grill the burger buns until they are toasty and just beginning to crisp up while the mushrooms are roasting.

7. To assemble the burgers, put a grilled portobello mushroom on the bottom of each toasted burger bun. Top with your preferred burger ingredients: lettuce, tomato,

red onion, avocado, mayo, mustard, or ketchup slices. Place the remaining bun on top.

8. Serve: Present the grilled portobello mushroom burgers immediately and any extra sides and condiments you choose.

NOTE:

➤ Including herbs or spices like smoky paprika, rosemary, or thyme in the marinade can enhance the mushrooms' flavor.

➤ You are welcome to alter the condiments and toppings to suit your tastes.

➤ Enjoying these burgers right off the grill, with the mushrooms juicy and hot, is optimal.

29. BEER CAN CHICKEN

INGREDIENTS:

- ❖ 1 whole chicken (about 4-5 pounds)
- ❖ 1 can of beer (any variety, half-full)
- ❖ 2 tablespoons olive oil or melted butter
- ❖ 2 tablespoons BBQ rub or seasoning blend
- ❖ Salt and black pepper to taste
- ❖ Optional: additional seasonings like garlic powder, onion powder, paprika, etc.

INSTRUCTIONS:

1. Grill Preparation: Heat your grill to medium-high in preparation for indirect cooking. Place the coals on one side of a charcoal barbecue to make a two-zone fire. When lighting a gas grill, light it from one side alone.
2. To prepare the chicken, remove the giblets (if any are present) from the cavity and pat it dry with paper towels. Use your preferred seasonings, along with salt and black

pepper, to coat the chicken from the inside out. To make the skin of the chicken crisp up while cooking, coat it completely with melted butter or olive oil.

3. Crack Open the Beer Can: Squeeze a few sips (or roughly half of the contents) from the beer can. The can should be halfway full. Optional: For added flavor, you can add more seasonings or aromatics to the beer, including chopped garlic, sliced onions, or fresh herbs.

4. Establish the Beer Can: Place the chicken atop the partially filled beer can. Once the can is placed within the cavity, the bird should sit erect. The legs should be pointed downward to form a sturdy tripod.

5. Grill the Chicken: Set the grill over the indirect heat zone and place the beer-can chicken on it. Verify that the chicken is securely in place and will not fall over. After 1.5 to 2 hours of uncovered boiling, or when the fluids drain clean, remove the lid. At this time, the chicken should reach an internal temperature of 165°F (75°C).

6. Relax and Prepare: Use oven mitts, tongs, or a sturdy spatula to carefully remove the chicken off the grill once it is cooked. Peel the beer can gently (it becomes hot!) after the chicken has rested for 10 minutes. Accompany the carved chicken with extra fixings, such as sides or BBQ sauce.

NOTE:

➢ Throughout cooking, monitor the grill's temperature and adjust the heat as necessary to keep it there.

➢ Because the beer can and the chicken will both be hot, you should always handle the beer can chicken cautiously to prevent burns.

➢ You can use a customized beer can chicken holder to simplify supporting the chicken on the grill.

30. BBQ PORK CHOPS

INGREDIENTS:

- ❖ 4 pork chops with the bone in, approximately 1 inch thick
- ❖ Salt and black pepper to taste
- ❖ 1 cup BBQ sauce (homemade or store-bought)
- ❖ 2 tablespoons olive oil
- ❖ 2 cloves garlic, minced (optional)
- ❖ 1 teaspoon paprika
- ❖ 1/2 teaspoon cayenne pepper (optional for added heat)
- ❖ Fresh parsley for garnish (optional)

INSTRUCTIONS:

1. Get your grill ready by heating it to a medium-high temperature, approximately 375–400°F (190–200°C). Make sure the grates are spotless and lightly greased
2. to keep them from sticking.

3. Pork chops should be set aside. Gently pat them dry with paper towels. Season the pork chops with salt & pepper, making sure to coat both sides.

4. To prepare the barbecue sauce, place the olive oil in a small saucepan and place it over medium heat. For about one minute, or until the minced garlic starts to release its scent, sauté it. Incorporate the paprika, BBQ sauce, and cayenne pepper (if preferred) and combine thoroughly. Simmer, stirring periodically, for 5 to 7 minutes until the sauce has thickened slightly, on medium heat. Keep at a cool temperature.

5. Grill the pork chops until they get a golden brown color, after seasoning them with salt and pepper. For the next five to six minutes, repeat on the other side.

6. Brush the prepared BBQ sauce generously over the top surfaces of the pork chops after grilling for five or six minutes on each side. Coat the underside of the pork chops with BBQ sauce once you've flipped them.

7. Keep up the good work A meat thermometer put into the thickest part of the pork chop should read 145°F (63°C) for medium-rare or medium-cook doneness, so continue grilling the chops for another five or six minutes.

8. Once the pork chops are cooked through and coated with BBQ sauce, take them off the grill and give them a few minutes to rest before cutting into them. Garnish with parsley if desired.

NOTE:

➢ It is essential to modify the cooking duration of your pork chops based on their thickness to guarantee that they are thoroughly cooked without losing their juicy texture.

➢ You can alter the taste of BBQ sauce by adding vinegar, honey, mustard, or Worcestershire sauce.

➢ Use a smoker or top your grill with a few wood chips for a smokier taste.

31. CHIPOTLE BBQ CHICKEN SKEWERS

INGREDIENTS:

- ❖ Cubes of 1.5 pounds (680 grams) of boneless, skinless chicken breasts
- ❖ To keep wooden skewers from burning, soak them in water for half an hour.
- ❖ a half-cup of barbecue sauce
- ❖ Two chopped chipotle peppers in adobo
- ❖ and two tablespoons of the chipotle peppers' sauce
- ❖ 2 tablespoons olive oil
- ❖ 2 cloves garlic, minced
- ❖ 1 teaspoon smoked paprika
- ❖ 1 teaspoon ground cumin
- ❖ 1/2 teaspoon dried oregano
- ❖ Salt and black pepper to taste
- ❖ Fresh cilantro for garnish (optional)

INSTRUCTION:

1. Add the olive oil, ground cumin, dried oregano, smoked paprika, minced chipotle peppers, adobo sauce, BBQ sauce, salt, and black pepper

2. to a bowl to make the marinade.

3. Marinate the chicken by placing the chopped breasts in a shallow dish or a securely sealed plastic bag. Be careful to coat the chicken completely after pouring the marinade over it. To let the flavors blend, cover the dish or place it in a sealed bag and refrigerate for at least 30 minutes or up to 4 hours.

4. How to Prepare the Grill: Turn the grill to medium-high heat.

5. Gather the Skewers: Thread the marinated chicken cubes onto the wet wooden skewers, making sure to leave a tiny space between each piece. This will ensure consistent cooking.

6. Set the grill to high heat and prepare the skewers by placing the chicken skewers on it. Sear the chicken for 5–7 minutes on each side for medium-rare doneness. Brush it with any remaining marinade, if any, at regular intervals.

7. When the chicken skewers are done cooking, take them off the grill and set them on a platter to serve. Add fresh cilantro as a garnish if you like. With additional BBQ sauce available for dipping, serve the meal hot.

8. Serve: After the chicken skewers are well cooked, remove them from the grill and place them on a serving plate. If desired, garnish with fresh cilantro. Serve the dish hot, providing extra BBQ sauce for dipping on the side.

NOTE:

- ➢ To avoid grill burns, soak wooden skewers in water for 30 minutes before grilling.
- ➢ If you like your marinade hotter, you can increase the amount of minced chipotle peppers or adobo sauce.
- ➢ These skewers are excellent as appetizers or served with a side salad, grilled veggies, or rice.

INGREDIENTS:

For the Chicken:

- ❖ 4 bone-in, skin-on chicken pieces (such as breasts, thighs, or drumsticks)
- ❖ Salt and black pepper to taste
- ❖ Olive oil for brushing

For the Alabama White Sauce:

- ❖ 1 cup mayonnaise
- ❖ 1/4 cup apple cider vinegar
- ❖ 2 tablespoons prepared horseradish
- ❖ 1 tablespoon lemon juice
- ❖ 1 teaspoon Worcestershire sauce
- ❖ 1 teaspoon Dijon mustard
- ❖ 1/2 teaspoon garlic powder
- ❖ 1/2 teaspoon onion powder

- ❖ 1/2 teaspoon smoked paprika
- ❖ 1/4 teaspoon cayenne pepper (optional for heat)
- ❖ Salt and black pepper to taste

INSTRUCTIONS:

1. Get the grill up to a medium-high heat (around 190–200°C, or 375–400°F) before you use it.
2. Rub some spices on the chicken. After washing the chicken, pat it dry with paper towels. Coat both sides with a generous amount of salt and black pepper.
3. Coat the grill grates gently with olive oil to prevent them from sticking while you grill the chicken. Skin side down, put the marinated chicken breasts on the grill. Breasts should be grilled for 5–7 minutes per side, or until golden brown and skin is crisp, and internal temperature reaches 165°F (75°C), while thighs and drumsticks should be grilled for 175°F (80°C). Carefully turning the chicken over every so often will ensure even cooking.
4. Whip up the Alabama White Sauce: A medium-sized bowl is ideal for combining the following ingredients: mayonnaise, horseradish, lemon juice, Dijon mustard, apple cider vinegar, Worcestershire sauce, smoked paprika, garlic powder, onion powder, and cayenne pepper (if utilizing). Salt and black pepper can be added according to taste. Adjust the spices according to your preference.
5. To serve, take the chicken off the grill after it's done cooking and let it aside to rest for a few minutes. With the Alabama white sauce on the side, serve the grilled

chicken with the option to dip it or drizzle it. Applying a little of the sauce to the chicken during its last minutes of grilling can enhance its taste even further.

6. Not required: For an extra splash of color and zest, top with freshly chopped parsley or chives just before serving.

NOTE:

➢ Alabama white sauce goes well with chicken, but it's versatile enough to accent salads or dip grilled meats in.

➢ Remaining leftover Alabama white sauce for up to seven days in the fridge is possible with an airtight container.

33. BBQ BACON-WRAPPED ASPARAGUS

INGREDIENTS:

- ❖ 1 pound (about 450g) fresh asparagus spears, tough ends trimmed
- ❖ 8-10 slices of bacon, cut in half crosswise
- ❖ BBQ sauce for brushing
- ❖ Salt and black pepper to taste
- ❖ Toothpicks or skewers (if needed)

INSTRUCTIONS:

1. Before using the grill, preheat it to a medium-high temperature (between 375 and 400°F, or 190 and 200°C).
2. Get the asparagus ready: After washing, cut off the tough ends of the asparagus spears. Using paper towels, pat dry the areas.
3. The asparagus spears should be firmly wrapped. Start at the bottom of the spears and work your way up to the tip

with a half-slice of bacon. If needed, use a toothpick or skewer to hold the bacon in place.

4. Season the Wrapped Asparagus: If preferred, season the asparagus wrapped in bacon with a dash of salt and black pepper. You can alter the amount of saltiness to suit your taste, as the bacon will add some.

5. Asparagus on the Grill: Lay the asparagus wrapped in bacon directly onto the grill grates. Grill, rotating periodically, for 8 to 10 minutes or until the asparagus is crisp-tender and the bacon is crispy.

6. Brush with BBQ Sauce: For the final few minutes of grilling, drizzle your preferred BBQ sauce over the bacon-wrapped asparagus. To guarantee uniform coating, turn them every so often.

7. Serve: After grilling the asparagus and bacon until they reach the desired crispiness and doneness, transfer them to a serving platter. As an appetiser or side dish, serve hot.

NOTE:

➤ You can alter this recipe by sprinkling the asparagus with your preferred seasonings before encasing them in bacon. For added flavor, try smoked paprika, garlic powder, onion powder, or a small amount of cayenne pepper.

➤ Grill the wooden skewers after soaking them in water for half an hour. They will be protected from burning by this.

➤ You are welcome to serve extra BBQ sauce on the side to dip alongside the asparagus wrapped in bacon.

INGREDIENTS:

For the BBQ Pork:

- ❖ 1 pound (about 450g) pork tenderloin or pork shoulder, thinly sliced
- ❖ 1/4 cup soy sauce
- ❖ 2 tablespoons hoisin sauce
- ❖ 2 tablespoons honey or brown sugar
- ❖ 2 cloves garlic, minced
- ❖ One tablespoon of apple cider vinegar or rice vinegar
- ❖ One tablespoon of vegetable oil
- ❖ 1 teaspoon five-spice powder (optional)
- ❖ Salt and black pepper to taste

For the Sandwiches:

- ❖ Baguettes or French rolls split lengthwise

- ❖ Mayonnaise or aioli
- ❖ Pickled daikon and carrots (see recipe below)
- ❖ Fresh cilantro leaves
- ❖ Thinly sliced jalapeños or chili peppers
- ❖ Sliced cucumber
- ❖ Sliced ripe tomatoes
- ❖ Sriracha or chili sauce (optional)
- ❖ Pickled Daikon and Carrots:
- ❖ 1 large daikon radish, julienned
- ❖ 2 large carrots, julienned
- ❖ 1 cup rice vinegar
- ❖ 1/4 cup sugar
- ❖ 1 tablespoon salt

INSTRUCTIONS:

1. To marinate the pork, put the soy sauce, hoisin sauce, brown sugar or honey, rice vinegar, vegetable oil, chopped garlic, salt, and black pepper in a bowl.
2. After adding the thinly sliced pork to the marinade, make sure the meat is well coated. Let the flavors marry, cover, and chill for at least an hour, but it is better overnight.
3. Get the carrots and daikon ready for pickling:
4. Put the sugar, salt, and rice vinegar into a small saucepan and stir to combine. Melt the sugar and salt by stirring constantly over low heat.
5. Prepare a sterile jar with julienned carrots and daikon radish. Pour hot vinegar over the vegetables and stir to coat.

6. Mix the flavors by letting the pickled carrots and daikon cool to room temperature, then cover and chill for at least an hour, ideally all night.
7. Fire up the Barbecued Pork:
8. Set your grill's temperature to medium-high. Take the pork that has been marinated out of the fridge and allow it to come to room temperature.
9. Either skewer or cook the pork slices directly on the prepared grill. Cook the pork for 3–4 minutes on each side or until it's well done and has excellent grill marks. Remove the pork from the grill and give it some time to rest.
10. Put the Sandwiches Together:
11. Cut the French rolls or baguettes lengthwise, leaving one side whole. Coat the inside of each bun with aioli or mayonnaise.
12. Inside the sandwiches, arrange the thinly sliced jalapeños or chili peppers, pickled daikon and carrots, sliced tomatoes, sliced cucumber, and fresh cilantro leaves.
13. If desired, drizzle with chili or Sriracha sauce.
14. Enjoy your delectable BBQ pork banh mi sandwiches right away after serving!

NOTE:

➤ You can change the condiments and toppings to suit your tastes. Avocado slices, lettuce, and a sprinkle of soy sauce or fish sauce for taste are more alternatives.

➤ You may also cook the BBQ pork in an oven or pan if you don't have a barbecue. As a result, modify the cooking time.

➤ You may keep leftover pickled carrots and daikon in the fridge for up to a week. They are a delicious garnish for salads, rice bowls, and sandwiches.

INGREDIENTS:

For the Burgers:

- ❖ Ground beef, ideally an 80/20 mix, 1 and 1/4 pounds
- ❖ Salt and black pepper to taste
- ❖ 4 hamburger buns, split
- ❖ Lettuce leaves
- ❖ Sliced tomatoes
- ❖ Sliced red onions
- ❖ Pickles (optional)

For the Smoked Gouda BBQ Sauce:

- ❖ 1 cup BBQ sauce (your favorite variety)
- ❖ 4 slices smoked Gouda cheese

INSTRUCTIONS:

1. To make the Smoked Gouda BBQ Sauce, put it in a small pot and reheat it over medium-low heat. While you make the burgers, keep them heated on the stovetop.

2. Form the Burger Patties: Using four equal pieces of ground beef, form each into a slightly bigger patty than the hamburger buns. Using your thumb, make a small dimple in the center of each patty to keep them from rising while cooking. Add a little salt and black pepper to each side of the burger.

3. Set the Grill's Temperature to Medium-High: Set the grill's temperature between 375 and 400°F (190 and 200°C). To avoid sticking, make sure the grates are spotless and lightly oiled.

4. Cook the Burgers: After the grill has heated up, place the burger patties on it and cook them for four to five minutes on each side or until they are cooked to your preference. During the final minute of grilling, put a slice of smoked Gouda cheese on top of each burger, then cover the grill to let the cheese melt.

5. Toast the Burger Buns: Put the hamburger buns on the grill, cut side down, and toast them for one to two minutes, or until they are just beginning to turn golden brown, while the burgers are cooking.

6. Assemble the Burgers: Top each toasted bread half with a grilled burger patty. Place a dollop of the reheated smoked Gouda BBQ sauce over each patty.

7. Add the lettuce leaves, sliced tomatoes, sliced red onions, and pickles (if using) to the BBQ sauce.

8. To finish the burgers, place the upper portion of the bun over the toppings.
9. Serve: Present the smoked Gouda BBQ burgers right away, along with an additional serving of BBQ sauce for dipping or drizzling.

NOTE:

➢ To top your burger just the way you like it, choose from caramelized onions, sautéed mushrooms, avocado slices, or crispy bacon.

➢ You can skip the grilling and just cook the burgers in a pan or skillet over medium-high heat in the stovetop. If necessary, modify the cooking time.

➢ If you want your burgers to keep their juicy, delicious texture, don't cook them for too long. Take the internal temperature of the ground beef with a meat thermometer to make sure it's cooked all the way through. The ideal temperature is 71 degrees Celsius, or 160 degrees Fahrenheit.

INGREDIENTS:

For the BBQ Chicken:

- ❖ 2 boneless, skinless chicken breasts
- ❖ 1 cup BBQ sauce (your favorite variety)
- ❖ 2 tablespoons olive oil
- ❖ 1 tablespoon honey or brown sugar (optional)
- ❖ 1 teaspoon smoked paprika
- ❖ 1/2 teaspoon garlic powder
- ❖ Salt and black pepper to taste

For the Sweet Potatoes:

- ❖ 4 medium sweet potatoes
- ❖ 1 tablespoon olive oil
- ❖ Salt and black pepper to taste

For Serving:

- ❖ To garnish, you can use chopped green onions or fresh cilantro, just to taste.
- ❖ Sour cream or Greek yogurt (optional)

INSTRUCTIONS:

1. Turn on the Oven: Set the oven's temperature to 400°F or 200°C.
2. Get the sweet potatoes ready by:
3. After you scrub the sweet potatoes, blot them dry with a paper towel. To release steam while baking, pierce sweet potatoes several times with a knife or fork. Sprinkle some salt and black pepper on top of the sweet potatoes after lightly coating them with olive oil.After lining a baking sheet with foil or parchment paper
4. , set aside.
5. For the best results, bake sweet potatoes: Put the baking sheet in the oven with the potatoes to warm it up. After 45 to 60 minutes in the oven, a fork should go into one and reveal tenderness.
6. While the sweet potatoes are baking, get the chicken for the BBQ. Combine the smoked paprika, olive oil, BBQ sauce, garlic powder, salt, black pepper, and honey or brown sugar (if using) in a basin. Half a cup of the barbecue sauce should be set aside for later use.
7. The chicken breasts can be stored in either a baking dish or a plastic bag that can be sealed. Coat the chicken thoroughly by tossing it in the leftover BBQ sauce.

Marinating the chicken for at least 30 minutes in the fridge

8. is a decent place to start, but at least 4 hours is better.
9. Take the chicken out of the refrigerator and allow it to reach room temperature before grilling. While you wait, get a skillet or grill up to medium heat.
10. The chicken should be opaque and grill-tender after 6 to 8 minutes per side, with no pink juices left over. Roasting the chicken for 20–25 minutes at 400°F (200°C)is another option.
11. Prior to shredding with two forks, let the chicken to rest for a few minutes after cooking.
12. In order to
13. put together the stuffed sweet potatoes, after they have baked and the BBQ chicken has been shred
14. ded, cut each potato lengthwise along the middle without cutting through.
15. Inspect the sweet potato and use a fork to fluff its inside. Divide the shredded BBQ chicken
16. among the sweet potatoes and stuff each one halfway.
17. Drizzle the reserved BBQ sauce over the piled sweet potatoes.
18. Fresh cilantro or freshly chopped green onions are optional garnishes.

Serve

- To serve, top the sweet potatoes packed with BBQ chicken with a dollop of sour cream or Greek yogurt, whichever you like.

NOTE:

➤ Feel free to alter the toppings to suit your preferences. You can top with your favorite toppings, such as chopped bacon, diced avocado, or grated cheese.

➤ These stuffed sweet potatoes make a filling and healthy meal. You may serve them with steamed veggies or a side salad for a complete dinner.

INGREDIENTS:

For the Chicken Marinade:

- ❖ 4 boneless, skinless chicken breasts
- ❖ 1 cup teriyaki sauce (store-bought or homemade)
- ❖ 1/4 cup pineapple juice
- ❖ 2 cloves garlic, minced
- ❖ 2 tablespoons soy sauce
- ❖ 2 tablespoons brown sugar
- ❖ 1 tablespoon olive oil
- ❖ Salt and black pepper to taste

For Grilling:

- ❖ Pineapple slices (fresh or canned)
- ❖ Olive oil or cooking spray for grilling

For Serving:

- ❖ Cooked white or brown rice
- ❖ Toss in some chopped cilantro or green onions for garnish, if you want.
- ❖ For garnish, if desired, sesame seeds

INSTRUCTIONS:

1. To make the chicken marinade, mix the teriyaki sauce, pineapple juice, soy sauce, brown sugar, olive oil, salt, and black pepper.
2. To marinate chicken, put the breasts in a plastic bag that can be sealed tightly or in a shallow dish. After pouring the marinade over the chicken, ensure it is evenly coated. Cover the dish or seal the bag and chill for at least 30 minutes or up to 4 hours to enable the flavors to mingle.
3. Warm up the grill:
4. Set your grill's temperature to medium-high, around 375–400°F (190–200°C). To avoid sticking, ensure the grill grates are clean and lightly greased.
5. The chicken should be removed from the marinade and placed aside before grilling. To get a chicken breast internal temperature of 165 degrees Fahrenheit (75 degrees Celsius), grill for 6 to 8 minutes per side. The cooking time for chicken breasts is proportional to their thickness.
6. Grill the Pineapple: Lightly brush or mist the pineapple slices with cooking spray or olive oil while the chicken roasts. Grill the pineapple slices on each side for two to

tree minutes until they are slightly caramelized and have excellent grill markings.

7. Serve: Remove the pineapple slices from the grill after they are grilled and the chicken is thoroughly cooked.
8. Overcooked rice, served with grilled teriyaki pineapple BBQ chicken.
9. If desired, garnish with chopped sesame seeds and green onions or cilantro.
10. Enjoy and serve right now!

NOTE:

➢ You can grill canned pineapple rings or fresh pineapple slices. Before cooking canned pineapple, be sure to drain it well.
➢ You can change the sweetness of the marinade to suit your taste by varying the amount of brown sugar added.
➢ If you put leftover grilled teriyaki pineapple BBQ chicken in an airtight container, it can be kept in the fridge for up to three to four days. This is perfect for meal prep or reheating leftovers.

37. BBQ BEEF KABOBS

INGREDIENTS:

- ❖ 1 1/2 lbs (680g) beef sirloin or tenderloin, cut into 1-inch cubes
- ❖ 1/4 cup (60ml) soy sauce
- ❖ 1/4 cup (60ml) olive oil
- ❖ 2 tablespoons Worcestershire sauce
- ❖ 2 tablespoons honey
- ❖ 2 cloves garlic, minced
- ❖ 1 teaspoon smoked paprika
- ❖ 1/2 teaspoon black pepper
- ❖ 1/2 teaspoon salt
- ❖ 1 red bell pepper, cut into chunks
- ❖ 1 green bell pepper, cut into chunks
- ❖ 1 red onion, cut into chunks
- ❖ Optional: Cherry tomatoes, mushrooms, zucchini, or any other vegetables of your choice

INSTRUCTIONS:

1. To make marinade, combine soy sauce, olive oil, Worcestershire sauce, honey, smoked paprika, black pepper, and salt in a medium-sized bowl.

2. Toss the meat cubes into a shallow dish or a large resealable plastic bag. Pour the marinade over the steak to ensure it is completely covered. To let the flavors marry, cover the dish or seal the bag, then chill it in the refrigerator for at least an hour, or even better, overnight.

3. To avoid burning while grilling, soak wooden skewers in water for half an hour.

4. Preheat the grill to a medium-high temperature.

5. Stuff the skewers with alternating threads of marinated beef cubes and onion, bell pepper, and any other vegetable leftovers you may have.

6. Once the grill is hot, brush a little oil on the grates to keep them from sticking. While the meat is cooking for 8 to 10 minutes, or until done to your liking, flip the skewers over one or twice. The veggies should be soft and gently browned.

7. Once done grilling, set the kabobs aside to cool for a bit before serving.

8. Refreshing salad, grilled veggies, rice, or your choice of side dish—served hot.

NOTE:

- ➢ If you want more flavor, add more herbs or spices to the marinade, such as thyme, rosemary, or chili flakes.
- ➢ To give the kabobs a sweet and tangy touch, add pineapple pieces to them.
- ➢ To achieve consistent cooking, leave some space on the skewers between the vegetables and the beef.
- ➢ Metal skewers can become quite hot when grilling, so proceed with caution. To handle them carefully, put them on a grill or oven mitts.

38. CAROLINA STYLE PULLED PORK

INGREDIENTS:

For the Pork:

- ❖ 4-5 lbs (about 2-2.5 kg) pork shoulder or pork butt
- ❖ 2 tablespoons brown sugar
- ❖ 2 tablespoons paprika
- ❖ 1 tablespoon garlic powder
- ❖ 1 tablespoon onion powder
- ❖ 1 tablespoon salt
- ❖ 1 teaspoon black pepper
- ❖ 1 cup apple cider vinegar
- ❖ 1 cup chicken broth or water
- ❖ 1 onion, chopped

For the Sauce:

- ❖ 1 cup apple cider vinegar
- ❖ 1/2 cup ketchup
- ❖ 1/4 cup brown sugar

- ❖ 2 tablespoons yellow mustard
- ❖ 1 tablespoon Worcestershire sauce
- ❖ 1 teaspoon hot sauce (adjust to taste)
- ❖ Salt and black pepper to taste

INSTRUCTIONS:

Get the pork ready:

1. To make a dry rub, combine the brown sugar, paprika, onion, garlic, and black pepper powders in a small bowl.
2. Make sure the pork shoulder is completely covered with the dry rub. Let it rest in the refrigerator for at least an hour or all night for optimal flavor.

Cooking the Pork:

1. Bring the oven temperature up to 325°F, or 160°C.
2. In a Dutch oven or roasting pan, arrange the chopped onion on the bottom. On top of the onions, lay the seasoned pork shoulder.
3. Toss the pork shoulder with a mixture of apple cider vinegar, chicken stock, or water.
4. Make sure the pan is completely covered by using the lid or aluminum foil.
5. After four or five hours in the oven, the pig should be extremely tender and readily shredded with a fork.
6. The pork should be given a 15 to 20 minute rest period once it is taken out of the oven
7. Start the Sauce: While the pork is resting, start the Carolina-style barbecue sauce.

8. Combine the following ingredients in a saucepan: apple cider vinegar, ketchup, brown sugar, mustard, Worcestershire sauce, spicy sauce, salt, and black pepper.
9. Stir the ingredients occasionally while simmering in a medium saucepan.
10. Keep the sauce simmering for 10–15 minutes, or until it thickens. Adjust the seasoning by tasting, if needed.

Pulling the Pork:

1. Shred the cooked pork shoulder into bite-sized pieces with two forks, removing any extra fat.
2. Spoon the pork shreds onto a dish or serving tray.

Serving suggestion:

1. Present the pulled pork with the made Carolina-style barbecue sauce on the side, letting guests drizzle on as much or as little as they choose.
2. Savor the pulled pork as a sandwich filler on bread with pickles and coleslaw.

NOTE:

➤ White bread, buns, and coleslaw are the customary accompaniments for pulled pork prepared in the Carolina style.
➤ For extended storage, pull pork leftovers can be frozen or kept in the refrigerator for up to three to four days in an airtight container.

39. BBQ CAULIFLOWER BITES

INGREDIENTS:

- ❖ 1 large head of cauliflower, cut into bite-sized florets
- ❖ 1 cup BBQ sauce (homemade or store-bought)
- ❖ 1/4 cup olive oil
- ❖ 2 tablespoons soy sauce
- ❖ 2 cloves garlic, minced
- ❖ 1 teaspoon smoked paprika
- ❖ 1/2 teaspoon chili powder
- ❖ Salt and black pepper, to taste
- ❖ Dip the vegetables in ranch or blue cheese, if desired.

INSTRUCTIONS:

1. Start the Oven and Preheat it to 450°F (230°C). Cooking spray or parchment paper should be lightly used to coat a baking sheet.
2. Prepare the cauliflower:
3. Once the cauliflower has been thoroughly washed, slice it into small pieces and discard the tough stems.
4. Olive oil, soy sauce, smoky paprika, minced garlic, chili powder, salt, and black pepper, along with the cauliflower florets, should be combined in a big mixing basin. Toss the cauliflower around so all of the sides are covered with the spice blend.
5. Arrange the seasoned cauliflower florets on a parchment-lined baking pan. Leave the oven on until it's done.
6. While the meat is cooking for 8 to 10 minutes, or until done to your liking, flip the skewers over one or twice. The veggies should be soft and gently browned.
7. After the cauliflower is done cooking, place it in a separate, clean bowl
8. and drizzle with the BBQ sauce.
9. After the cauliflower florets have roasted, toss them in the BBQ sauce to coat them evenly.
10. Return the baking pan to the oven and uniformly distribute the cauliflower that has been coated.
11. After five to ten minutes in the oven, the BBQ sauce will have caramelized and become sticky.
12. Take the BBQ cauliflower chunks out of the oven and let them cool before serving.
13. These are delicious as an appetizer or snack when served hot with a side of blue cheese or ranch dressing.

NOTE:

➢ You can change the quantity of BBQ sauce to suit your tastes. Use less sauce if you want it to be lighter or more sauce if you want it to be saucier.

➢ Feel free to add your preferred herbs and spices to the seasoning combination for extra taste.

40. HONEY MUSTARD BBQ GLAZED CHICKEN

INGREDIENTS:

- ❖ 4 boneless, skinless chicken breasts
- ❖ Salt and black pepper, to taste
- ❖ 1/4 cup honey
- ❖ 2 tablespoons Dijon mustard
- ❖ 2 tablespoons barbecue sauce (homemade or store-bought)
- ❖ 1 tablespoon olive oil
- ❖ 2 cloves garlic, minced
- ❖ 1 teaspoon smoked paprika
- ❖ 1/2 teaspoon onion powder
- ❖ Optional: Fresh parsley for garnish

INSTRUCTIONS:

1. Heat the Grill: Set your grill to medium-high. Ensure the grates are clean, and give them a little oil to avoid sticking.

Get the chicken ready by:

2. Dredge the chicken breasts in salt and pepper, seasoning both sides according to taste.
3. The BBQ Honey Mustard Glaze needs to be prepared:
4. In a small bowl, whisk together the honey, Dijon mustard, barbecue sauce, smoking paprika, onion powder, and minced garlic until well combined.

After seasoning the chicken, grill it:

1. To avoid sticking, gently coat the chicken breasts with olive oil.
2. Sear the seasoned chicken breasts for five or six minutes per side on a preheated grill, or until they are nearly done.

Apply the Glaze:

1. By generously brushing the honey mustard BBQ glaze on during the last few minutes of grilling, the chicken breasts will be caramelized slightly on both sides.
2. After the chicken is cooked and the glaze has turned sticky and caramelized, continue grilling it on each side for one to two minutes.
3. After cooking, take the glazed chicken breasts from the grill and place them on a dish for serving.
4. Garnish with parsley, if preferred.

5. Warm-up and pair with your preferred side dishes, like grilled veggies, rice, or a crisp salad.

NOTE

➢ To keep the chicken from burning, keep a careful eye on it while grilling and adjust the heat as needed.

➢ Alternatively to grilling, baking the chicken is also an option. Just get the oven up to 375°F, or 190°C, and get the chicken ready. After 20–25 minutes in the oven, glaze the chicken and return it to the oven for 5–10 more minutes, or until done.

INGREDIENTS:

For the BBQ Chicken:

- ❖ 2 boneless, skinless chicken breasts
- ❖ Salt and black pepper, to taste
- ❖ 1 cup barbecue sauce (homemade or store-bought)

For the Salad:

- ❖ Six cups of mixed salad greens, including arugula, spinach, and romaine
- ❖ Half a cup of cherry tomatoes
- ❖ 1/2 cup frozen, canned, or fresh corn kernels
- ❖ Half a cup of rinsed and drained black beans
- ❖ 1/4 cup red onion, thinly sliced
- ❖ 1 avocado, diced
- ❖ 1/4 cup shredded cheddar cheese (optional)
- ❖ 1/4 cup chopped cilantro (optional)

For the Dressing:

- ❖ 1/4 cup barbecue sauce
- ❖ 2 tablespoons olive oil
- ❖ 1 tablespoon apple cider vinegar
- ❖ 1 teaspoon Dijon mustard
- ❖ Salt and black pepper, to taste

INSTRUCTIONS:

Grill Preparation:

1. Set your grill's temperature to medium-high.

Grill the Chicken:

1. Before you cook the chicken breasts, season them with salt and pepper.
2. The chicken breasts should be seasoned and cooked for 6 to 8 minutes per side, or until opaque throughout, once the grill is heated.
3. In the final minutes of grilling, brush the chicken breasts with the barbecue sauce to get a little caramelization on both sides. Take the chicken off the grill and let it rest for a while. Next, cut it into slices.

Get the Salad components Ready:

1. As the chicken grills, get the salad components ready.
2. If used, combine the mixed greens, cherry tomatoes, corn kernels, black beans, red onion, sliced avocado, shredded cheddar cheese, and chopped cilantro in a large salad dish and gently toss to mix.

3. Pour the dressing ingredients into a small bowl and whisk to combine. Add the barbecue sauce, Dijon mustard, apple cider vinegar, olive oil, salt, and black pepper.
4. After the BBQ chicken breasts have cooked, thinly slice them before you put the salad together.
5. After the chicken and vegetables are cooked, toss them with the salad.
6. After lightly spreading the dressing over the salad, toss it to coat it evenly.

Serve:

- Spoon the chicken salad with barbecue sauce onto separate bowls or plates.
- If desired, garnish with extra finely chopped cilantro.
- Enjoy and serve right now!

NOTE:

➤ Feel free to add your preferred toppings to the salad, such as shredded carrots, sliced bell peppers, or cucumber slices.
➤ To suit your taste, you can change the amount of barbecue sauce in the dressing. To have a more intense BBQ flavor, use more; add less to get a softer taste.

42. BBQ JACKFRUIT TACOS

INGREDIENTS:

For the BBQ Jackfruit:

- ❖ Twenty ounces of young green jackfruit per can, in water or brine; remove excess water and rinse.
- ❖ 1-cup barbecue sauce, either homemade or purchased
- ❖ 1 tablespoon olive oil
- ❖ 1/2 onion, finely chopped
- ❖ 2 cloves garlic, minced
- ❖ 1 teaspoon smoked paprika
- ❖ 1/2 teaspoon chili powder
- ❖ Salt and black pepper, to taste

For the Tacos:

- ❖ Eight small corn or flour tortillas
- ❖ 1 cup shredded cabbage or coleslaw mix

- ❖ 1/2 cup diced tomatoes
- ❖ 1/4 cup diced red onion
- ❖ 1/4 cup chopped cilantro
- ❖ Lime wedges for serving

INSTRUCTIONS:

1. To make the BBQ Jackfruit, shred the jackfruit chunks with a fork or your hands until they resemble pulled pork.
2. With the heat set to medium, warm the olive oil in a big skillet. Toss in the minced garlic and onion after a few minutesand keep cooking until they become soft.
3. Chili powder, smoked paprika, olive oil, salt, and black pepper should be sautéed with the shredded jackfruit. Thoroughly mix to combine.
4. Coat the jackfruit mixture with the barbecue sauce by tossing it well. After the jackfruit has been simmering for ten to fifteen minutes, or until heated through and flavors have blended, reduce heat to low and stir occasionally. To thin it out, add additional water or vegetable broth if it thickens too much.
5. To assemble the tacos, preheat the tortillas in a microwave or dry skillet per the directions on the package.
6. The BBQ jackfruit mixture should be spooned onto each tortilla.
7. Add chopped cilantro, tomatoes, red onion, and shredded cabbage or coleslaw mix on top.
8. Squeeze a lime wedge over the tacos right before you serve them.

Serve:

- Present the Barbecued Jackfruit tacos promptly with extra lime wedges on the side.
- Savor the tasty and succulent vegetarian or vegan tacos!

NOTE:

➤ You can alter the toppings to suit your tastes. Extra choices include vegan cheese, diced jalapeños for spiciness, sliced avocado or guacamole, or a drizzle of vegan sour cream or yogurt.

➤ You can adjust the spice level of the BBQ jackfruit by adding extra chili powder or a little hot sauce to the blend.

➤ Young green jackfruit is best used in water or brine, not syrup, as the syrupy kind is too sugary for savory recipes like tacos.

43. BBQ PORK SLIDERS WITH COLESLAW

INGREDIENTS:

For the BBQ Pork:

- ❖ 1 lb (450g) pork tenderloin or pork shoulder
- ❖ Salt and black pepper, to taste
- ❖ 1 cup barbecue sauce (homemade or store-bought)
- ❖ 1/4 cup chicken broth or water
- ❖ 1 tablespoon olive oil
- ❖ 1/2 onion, finely chopped
- ❖ 2 cloves garlic, minced
- ❖ Slider buns, for serving

For the Coleslaw:

- ❖ 2 cups shredded cabbage or coleslaw mix
- ❖ 1 carrot, grated
- ❖ 2 tablespoons mayonnaise
- ❖ 1 tablespoon apple cider vinegar

- ❖ 1 teaspoon honey or sugar
- ❖ Salt and black pepper, to taste

INSTRUCTIONS:

1. Season the pork tenderloin or shoulder with salt and black pepper on both sides before barbecuing it.
2. Melt the olive oil in a Dutch oven or skillet over medium heat. Sauté the minced and diced garlic and onion for three to four minutes or until they are tender and fragrant.
3. Put the spiced pork in a pan and brown it by searing it for a couple of minutes each side.
4. While the pork marinates in the skillet, add chicken stock (or water) and coat it with barbecue sauce. Simmer, covered, for 20–25 minutes (or until meat is tender), stirring once or twice.
5. Shred the pork with two forks after removing it from the pan.
6. To make the Coleslaw, grate the carrot and place the shredded cabbage or coleslaw mix in a mixing dish.
7. To make the coleslaw dressing, combine the mayonnaise, apple cider vinegar, honey (or sugar), salt, and black pepper in a small bowl.
8. After adding the dressing, toss the cabbage mixture until it is well coated. Taste and adjust the seasoning.
9. Put the sliders together by toasting the slider buns, if preferred.
10. Put a heaping spoonful of BBQ pork shreds on the lower portion of every slider bread.

11. Place a dollop of coleslaw on top of the pork.
12. To finish the sliders, place the top half of the slider bun on top of the coleslaw.

Serve:

- Put the BBQ Pork Sliders on a dish and start serving right away.
- Savor these mouthwatering sliders as a party snack or appetizer!

NOTE:

➢ To add even more flavor and crunch, feel free to add chopped cilantro, diced bell peppers, or sliced green onions to the coleslaw.
➢ You can modify the amount of barbecue sauce on the pork to suit your own tastes. For a saucier filling, use more; for a lighter coating, use less.

INGREDIENTS:

For the Jamaican Jerk Marinade:

- ❖ 4 bone-in, skin-on chicken thighs (or other chicken pieces of your choice)
- ❖ 2 tablespoons soy sauce
- ❖ 2 tablespoons olive oil
- ❖ 2 tablespoons brown sugar
- ❖ 2 tablespoons lime juice
- ❖ 2 cloves garlic, minced
- ❖ 1 tablespoon grated fresh ginger
- ❖ 1 tablespoon Jamaican jerk seasoning
- ❖ 1 teaspoon dried thyme
- ❖ 1 teaspoon allspice
- ❖ 1/2 teaspoon cinnamon
- ❖ 1/2 teaspoon black pepper

- ❖ 1/2 teaspoon saltAn extra item that can be used for spice is a minced and seeded Scotch bonnet or habanero pepper.

For the BBQ Glaze:

- ❖ 1/2 cup barbecue sauce (homemade or store-bought)
- ❖ 2 tablespoons honey
- ❖ 1 tablespoon lime juice
- ❖ 1 teaspoon Jamaican jerk seasoning

INSTRUCTIONS:

Get the Jamaican Jerk Marinade ready.

1. Mix soy sauce, olive oil, brown sugar, lime juice, grated ginger, minced garlic, dried thyme, allspice, cinnamon, black pepper, salt, and minced habanero or Scotch bonnet pepper (if using) in a bowl. To suit your tastes, turn up or down the heat.
2. The chicken thighs can be put in a big ziplock bag or a shallow plate. Before you pour the marinade over the chicken, make sure to coat each piece completely. Refrigerate for at least two hours, or even better, overnight, to allow the flavors to develop. Either seal the bag or cover the dish.
3. The BBQ Glaze is made by combining the barbecue sauce, honey, lime juice, and Jamaican jerk seasoning in a small skillet. Over medium heat, simmer the ingredients, stirring occasionally. After two or three minutes of simmering, remove from heat. Put aside.

Grill the Chicken:

1. Turn the heat up to medium-high on your grill.
2. After taking the marinated chicken out of the fridge, give it a good 20 to 30 minutes to come to room temperature.
3. Shake off any excess marinade before removing the chicken pieces and throwing away the leftover marinade.
4. Skin side down, place the chicken thighs on the heated grill. Take the chicken off the grill and put it back on after 5 to 6 minutes per side, or until the temperature inside reaches 165 degrees Fahrenheit (75 degrees Celsius) and it becomes white when pierced in the center.
5. In the last few minutes of cooking, brush the chicken thighs with the BBQ glaze on both sides. This will allow it to slightly caramelize. Make sure the glaze doesn't burn.
6. After the chicken has cooked through, remove it from the grill and let it rest for a while before cutting into it.

Serve:

- Top the Jamaican Jerk BBQ Chicken with sliced green onions or freshly chopped cilantro, if preferred.
- Savor the aromatic and delectable chicken with your preferred side dishes, such as Jamaican-style coleslaw, grilled veggies, or rice and peas.

NOTE:

- ➢ Even without a grill, a thorough baking of the chicken at 375°F (190°C) for 35 to 40 minutes will do the trick. In the middle of the cooking process, brush the chicken with the BBQ glaze.

45. SMOKED SAUSAGE AND PEPPER SKEWERS

INGREDIENTS:

- ❖ 1 lb (450g) smoked sausage, cut into 1-inch chunks
- ❖ 1 red bell pepper, cut into chunks
- ❖ 1 yellow bell pepper, cut into chunks
- ❖ 1 green bell pepper, cut into chunks
- ❖ 1 red onion, cut into chunks
- ❖ 2 tablespoons olive oil
- ❖ 2 cloves garlic, minced
- ❖ 1 teaspoon dried oregano
- ❖ 1 teaspoon smoked paprika
- ❖ Salt and black pepper, to taste
- ❖ Wooden or metal skewers

INSTRUCTIONS:

Prepare the Skewers:

1. To avoid burning while grilling, soak wooden skewers in water for approximately half an hour.
2. Leaving a small gap between each piece, thread the chunks of smoked sausage, bell pepper, and red onion onto the skewers in that order.
3. Marinade ingredients include olive oil, garlic powder, smoked paprika, dried oregano, salt, and black pepper. Combine all of these ingredients in a small bowl.

Skewers should be marinated:

1. Arrange the prepared skewers in a big plastic bag that can be sealed tightly or in a shallow dish.
2. Ensure that every skewer has an even coating of marinade when you pour the marinade over them. To disperse the marinade, gently massage the skewers with the bag if using one, then shut it.
3. To allow the flavors to mingle, place the skewers in the refrigerator and marinade them for at least half an hour.

Grill Preparation:

1. Set your grill's temperature to medium-high.

Grill the Skewers:

1. To keep the grates from sticking, lightly oil them when the grill has heated up.
2. Once the grill is hot, add the marinated skewers and cook, turning often, for 8 to 10 minutes, or until sausage is

cooked through and veggies are tender and slightly charred.

3. The time required to cook the sausage will vary according to its thickness and the temperature of the grill.

To serve:

- Take the grilled skewers from the grill and place them on a dish.
- Serve the spicy pepper skewers and smoked sausage as a flavorful first course or main course.
- Optional: Before serving, sprinkle some freshly chopped parsley or pour some lemon juice over top.

NOTE:

➢ Feel free to use different veggies, such cherry tomatoes, zucchini, or mushrooms, to personalize the skewers.

➢ For added flavor, you can also brush any leftover marinade over the skewers while they're grilling.

➢ If you would rather, you can bake the skewers for 20 to 25 minutes at 400°F (200°C), or until the vegetables are soft and the sausage is thoroughly cooked.

46. BBQ TURKEY MEATLOAF

INGREDIENTS:

- ❖ 1 lb (450g) ground turkey
- ❖ 1/2 cup breadcrumbs
- ❖ 1/4 cup barbecue sauce (plus extra for glazing)
- ❖ 1/4 cup grated Parmesan cheese
- ❖ one-fourth cup finely chopped onions
- ❖ one-fourth cup of chopped bell peppers–any color
- ❖ chopped celery, measuring 1/4 cup
- ❖ 2 cloves garlic, minced
- ❖ 1 large egg, beaten
- ❖ 1 tablespoon Worcestershire sauce
- ❖ 1 teaspoon dried thyme
- ❖ 1 teaspoon dried oregano
- ❖ 1/2 teaspoon smoked paprika
- ❖ Salt and black pepper, to taste
- ❖ Optional: Chopped parsley for garnish

INSTRUCTIONS:

1. Make sure the oven is warmed at 375°F (190°C) before you turn it on. Prepare a loaf pan by lightly greasing or spraying it with cooking spray.

Get the Meatloaf Combination Ready:

1. In a big mixing bowl, combine ground turkey, breadcrumbs, barbecue sauce, grated Parmesan cheese, diced bell pepper, diced onion, chopped celery, minced garlic, beaten egg, Worcestershire sauce, smoked paprika, dried thyme, and dried oregano.
2. Mix everything together thoroughly, either with a spoon or your hands. Avoid over-mixing the meatloaf, as this may cause it to become dense.

Form the Meatloaf:

1. Using a spoon, transfer batter into loaf pan that has been prepared. Using your hands, carefully push it into the shape of a loaf, being careful not to leave any air spaces.

Barbecue Sauce Glaze:

1. Evenly coat the entire surface of the meatloaf with more barbecue sauce.

Bake the Meatloaf:

2. After the oven has been warmed, place the loaf pan inside and bake for 45 to 50 minutes, or until the top of the meatloaf has turned golden brown.
3. A meat thermometer should be inserted into the center of the meatloaf to determine doneness. It ought to measure a minimum of 165°F, or 75°C.

4. After cooking, take the meatloaf out of the oven and allow it to rest in the loaf pan for ten minutes or so before slicing.
5. If desired, garnish with finely chopped parsley.
6. Cut the meatloaf into slices and serve hot, accompanied with your preferred sides, like roasted veggies, mashed potatoes, or a crisp salad.

NOTE:

➢ Feel free to use your preferred add-ins or ingredients, such as diced carrots, chopped mushrooms, or other herbs and spices, to personalize the meatloaf.
➢ Meatloaf leftovers keep well in the refrigerator for three to four days when kept in an airtight container. It freezes well as well for extended storage.

INGREDIENTS:

For the BBQ Chicken:

- ❖ 1 boneless, skinless chicken breast
- ❖ Salt and black pepper, to taste
- ❖ 1/2 cup barbecue sauce (homemade or store-bought)
- ❖ 1 tablespoon olive oil
- ❖ quarter cup of chopped red onion
- ❖ one-fourth cup of chopped bell peppers–any color
- ❖ 1/4 cup chopped pineapple, if desired
- ❖ 1/4 cup chopped cilantro (optional)
- ❖ 1 cup shredded mozzarella cheese

For the Flatbread Pizza:

- ❖ 2 flatbreads or pre-made pizza crusts
- ❖ Olive oil, for brushing
- ❖ 1/2 cup barbecue sauce (for pizza base)

- ❖ 1 cup shredded mozzarella cheese
- ❖ Thinly sliced red onion (optional)
- ❖ Thinly sliced jalapeños (optional)
- ❖ Chopped fresh cilantro (optional)

INSTRUCTIONS:

1. Before grilling the chicken breasts, season them with black pepper and salt.
2. In a pan or skillet set over medium-high heat, warm the olive oil. Put the chicken breasts in the pan when they are no longer pink in the center, and cook for a couple of minutes on each side.
3. After cooking, take the chicken out of the skillet and give it some time to rest. Next, using two forks, shred the chicken.
4. Combine the barbecue sauce and shredded chicken in a small bowl, stirring to coat the meat evenly. Put aside.
5. To put together the flatbread pizza, preheat the oven to 400°F, or 200°C.
6. Transfer the prepared pizza crusts or flatbreads to a parchment paper-lined baking sheet.
7. Lightly coat the flatbreads with olive oil.
8. Leaving a thin border all the way around, cover each flatbread with an equal amount of barbecue sauce.
9. Over the layer of barbecue sauce, scatter the shredded mozzarella cheese.
10. Evenly spread the combination of BBQ chicken over the top of cheese.

11. Distribute the diced pineapple, bell pepper, and red onion (if using) among the chicken pieces.
12. Add one more layer of shredded mozzarella cheese on top.
13. To bake the Flatbread Pizzas, preheat the oven, place the baking sheet inside, and bake for 10 to 12 minutes, or until the cheese is bubbling and melted and the flatbreads' edges are golden brown.

Serve:

- Take the baked flatbread pizzas out of the oven.
- Over the pizzas, scatter thinly sliced jalapeños and freshly chopped cilantro, if using.
- Pizzas should be served hot after being cut into wedges or squares.
- Savor your mouthwatering flatbread pizzas with BBQ chicken!

NOTE:

- ➢ Feel free to change the toppings to suit your tastes. Sliced mushrooms, cooked bacon, or any other preferred pizza toppings can be added.
- ➢ You can bake the flatbreads for a few minutes in advance before topping them for a crispier crust.

48. GRILLED BBQ CHICKEN DRUMSTICKS

INGREDIENTS:

- ❖ 8 chicken drumsticks
- ❖ Salt and black pepper, to taste
- ❖ 1 cup barbecue sauce (homemade or store-bought)
- ❖ Olive oil, for brushing
- ❖ As a garnish, you can add chopped fresh cilantro or parsley if you choose.

INSTRUCTIONS:

Get the chicken ready by:

1. Using paper towels, gently pat dry the chicken drumsticks. Give them a liberal amount of salt and black pepper on all sides.

Warm Up the Grill:

2. The ideal grill temperature is from 375 to 400 degrees Fahrenheit, or 200 to 375 degrees Celsius. Keep the grill grates clean and lightly greased to keep food from sticking.
3. Grill the Chicken Drumsticks: Lightly coat the drumsticks in olive oil to help them sear nicely on the grill and to keep them from sticking.
4. After heating the grill, place the drumsticks on it and cook them for 5 to 7 minutes on each side, flipping them from time to time, until they are browned and have grill marks.
5. Apply the Barbecue Sauce: Begin baste-frying the drumsticks with the sauce after they have browned. Distribute the sauce evenly over each drumstick using a brush.
6. Cook the drumsticks for a little while more, basting them with extra barbecue sauce and flipping them now and then, until they are cooked through. If you place a meat thermometer into the thickest portion of the drumstick, it should read 165°F (75°C) internally, and the juices should run clear.
7. After the drumsticks are thoroughly cooked and coated with barbecue sauce, take them off the grill and place them onto a dish for serving.
8. For a flare of color and flavor, feel free to garnish with chopped fresh parsley or cilantro.
9. Hot grilled BBQ chicken drumsticks go well with a variety of sides like grilled vegetables, coleslaw, potato salad, or corn on the cob.
10. Have a good time!

NOTE

➤ For a backyard barbecue or any informal event, grilled BBQ chicken drumsticks are ideal. They always bring a crowd and are quite simple to make!

49. BBQ TOFU SKEWERS

INGREDIENTS:

- ❖ 1 block (14-16 oz) firm or extra firm tofu
- ❖ 1/2 cup barbecue sauce (homemade or store-bought)
- ❖ 2 tablespoons olive oil
- ❖ 2 tablespoons soy sauce or tamari
- ❖ 1 tablespoon maple syrup or honey
- ❖ 1 teaspoon smoked paprika
- ❖ 1/2 teaspoon garlic powder
- ❖ 1/2 teaspoon onion powder
- ❖ Salt and black pepper, to taste
- ❖ Optional: Vegetables for skewering (bell peppers, onions, cherry tomatoes, mushrooms, zucchini, etc.)
- ❖ Wooden or metal skewers

INSTRUCTIONS:

1. Pat the tofu dry using a clean dish towel or paper towels after the water has drained. Use a gentle pressing motion to extract any additional moisture. A tofu press is another possibility.
2. After the tofu has drained, slice it into cubes or rectangles that are one inch long.

The BBQ

1. marinade requires sugar, olive oil, Smoked paprika, garlic powder, onion powder, and salt, black pepper should be mixed together in a small bowl.
2. Simply placing the cubes of tofu in a shallow dish or a large plastic bag is all it takes to marinate.
3. As you pour the marinade over the tofu, make sure to coat each piece completely.At this point, you can include the veggies into the marinade if you're using them.
4. Cover the dish or seal the bag and refrigerate for at least 30 minutes to let the flavors blend. Marinade the tofu in the fridge for at least an hour for the best flavor.
5. Cover the dish or seal the bag and refrigerate for at least 30 minutes to let the flavors blend. Marinade the tofu in the fridge for at least an hour for the best flavor.

Prepare the Skewers:

1. To avoid burning while grilling, soak wooden skewers in water for approximately half an hour.
2. If preferred, alternate the marinated tofu cubes on the skewers with veggies.
3. To grill the skewers, preheat the grill to a temperature of medium-high.

4. To keep the grill grates from sticking, lightly oil them.

5. After preheating the grill, place the tofu skewers on it and cook for 4–5 minutes on each side, or until the tofu is thoroughly roasted and gently toasted. If desired, brush with extra marinade while cooking.

6. After the tofu skewers are cooked to your preference, take them off the grill and place them on a serving plate.

7. Chop fresh herbs like cilantroor parsley to garnish.

8. Quinoa, rice, or grilled veggies can be served with BBQ tofu skewers.

9. Best wishes!

NOTE

> For both meat eaters and vegetarians, barbecued tofu skewers are a tasty and healthy choice. These are ideal for picnics and summer cookouts, or any time you're in the mood for something wonderful grilled!

50. SMOKED MAPLE GLAZED HAM

INGREDIENTS:

- ❖ 1 fully-cooked bone-in ham (8-10 pounds)
- ❖ 1 cup maple syrup
- ❖ 1/2 cup brown sugar
- ❖ 1/4 cup Dijon mustard
- ❖ 2 tablespoons apple cider vinegar
- ❖ 2 teaspoons smoked paprika
- ❖ 1 teaspoon ground cinnamon
- ❖ 1/2 teaspoon ground cloves
- ❖ 1/2 teaspoon ground nutmeg

INSTRUCTIONS:

1. To prepare the smoker, preheat it to 250°F (120°C) and use your preferred wood chips or chunks. Excellent woods to smoke ham are hickory, applewood, or maple.

Assemble the Ham:

2. Take out the ham from its package and use paper towels to gently dry.
3. Using a sharp knife, make 1/4-inch-deep scores on the ham's surface in a diamond pattern. This is going to facilitate the glaze seeping into the meat.
4. Prepare the Maple Glaze by combining the maple syrup, brown sugar, Dijon mustard, apple cider vinegar, smoked paprika, ground cloves, ground nutmeg, and ground cinnamon in a saucepan. Simmer the mixture over medium heat and stirring occasionally and until the sugar dissolves and the glaze smooths. Cool place.
5. The ham should be smoked by placing it directly on the smoker grate, sliced side down if necessary, or on a rack inside a disposable aluminum pan to collect any drips.
6. Once the ham achieves an internal temperature of 140°F (60°C), close the smoker cover and smoke it for approximately two to three hours. Throughout the smoking process, you can use a basting brush or spoon to occasionally brush the ham with the maple glaze.
7. Brush generously with the leftover maple glaze on the ham's surface after it reaches 140°F (60°C).
8. To allow the glaze to caramelize and the interior temperature to reach 145°F (63°C), raise the smoker temperature to 325°F (160°C) and cook for a further 30 minutes.
9. Rest and Serve: Take out the ham with a maple glaze and place it on a chopping board. Allow it to rest for 15-20 minutes under loose aluminum foil before slicing.

10. If preferred, drizzle any leftover pan glaze over the ham slices after slicing and serving warm.
11. Enjoy yourself!

NOTE

> The centerpiece of every holiday feast or special event might be the delectable ham with a maple glaze and smoke. With a lovely smoky aroma and a mouthwatering taste that combines sweet and savory notes, your visitors will be begging for more!

51. BBQ BACON WRAPPED JALAPENO POPPERS

INGREDIENTS:

- ❖ 12 fresh jalapeno peppers
- ❖ 6 slices of bacon, cut in half
- ❖ 8 oz cream cheese, softened
- ❖ 1 cup shredded cheddar cheese
- ❖ 1 teaspoon garlic powder
- ❖ 1 teaspoon onion powder
- ❖ 1/2 teaspoon smoked paprika
- ❖ 1/2 cup barbecue sauce
- ❖ Toothpicks

INSTRUCTIONS:

1. Grill Prep: Set your grill's temperature to medium-high, between 375 and 400 degrees Fahrenheit.
2. The jalapenos should be halved lengthwise, and their seeds and membranes should be spooned out before

preparation. Wear gloves to protect your hands from the heated oils.

3. To make the Cream Cheese Filling, in a mixing dish combine the melted cream cheese, crumbled cheddar, smoky paprika, onion powder, and garlic powder. Mix everything together until smooth.

4. Partially fill jalapeños. Distribute the cream cheese mixture evenly among the two halves of the jalapeño.

5. Wrap with Bacon: Using a toothpick, wrap a half slice of bacon around each packed jalapeño half.

6. Grill: Arrange the jalapeño poppers wrapped in bacon on the prepared grill. After 15–20 minutes of grilling, turning once, the bacon should be crispy and the peppers should be tender.

7. Brush the jalapeño poppers with barbecue sauce during the final few minutes of grilling so that it may slightly caramelize.

8. Serve: Take the poppers off the grill and place them on a serving plate once the bacon is crispy and cooked through. Enjoy while hot!

NOTE:

➢ To control the heat level of the jalapeño poppers, you can remove all of the seeds and membranes for a softer flavor or leave some of them intact for more spiciness.

➢ To keep the toothpicks from burning on the grill, be sure to soak them in water for about half an hour before using them.

- These jalapeño poppers wrapped in BBQ bacon are great for game days, get-togethers, and parties. Savor the flavorful fusion of smokey bacon, creamy cheese, and fiery peppers!

52. GRILLED BBQ CHICKEN SANDWICHES

INGREDIENTS:

- ❖ 4 boneless, skinless chicken breasts
- ❖ Salt and pepper to taste
- ❖ 1 cup barbecue sauce
- ❖ 4 burger buns
- ❖ 4 slices cheddar, pepper jack, or your favorite
- ❖ Top with lettuce, tomato and red onion, or pickles.

INSTRUCTIONS:

1. Grill Prep: Set your grill's temperature to medium-high, between 375 and 400 degrees Fahrenheit.
2. To prepare the chicken, season both sides of the chicken breasts with salt and pepper.
3. Toast Buns: Lightly toast the hamburger buns on the grill until they get golden brown while the chicken is roasting.

4. Assemble Sandwiches: Take the chicken off the grill after it's fully cooked and coated with barbecue sauce. On top of each chicken breast, place a slice of cheese and let it melt a little. After that, put the grilled chicken breasts with cheese on top of the toasted buns to make the sandwiches.

5. Add Toppings: Garnish the sandwiches with your preferred ingredients, such as pickles, lettuce, tomatoes, and red onions.

6. Serve: Enjoy the excellent smoky flavor of the grilled BBQ chicken sandwiches by serving them hot right away!

NOTE:

➢ Feel free to experiment with different barbecue sauces, such as sour, spicy, sweet, or smokey, to personalize these sandwiches.

➢ For added taste, feel free to top with more ingredients like caramelized onions, crispy bacon, or slices of avocado.

➢ For a simple and quick weeknight supper or a weekend get-together with friends and family, these grilled BBQ chicken sandwiches are ideal. Have fun!

INGREDIENTS:

- ❖ 4 large russet potatoes
- ❖ 1 lb ground beef
- ❖ 1 small onion, diced
- ❖ 2 cloves garlic, minced
- ❖ 1/2 cup barbecue sauce
- ❖ Salt and pepper to taste
- ❖ Shredded cheddar cheese for topping
- ❖ Chopped green onions for garnish (optional)
- ❖ Sour cream for serving (optional)

INSTRUCTIONS:

1. Set Oven Preparation: Set the oven temperature to 400°F, or 200°C.

2. Wash the russet potatoes and puncture them multiple times using a fork before baking. When a fork pierces them, they should be soft. Put them immediately into the oven rack and bake for 45 to 60 minutes.
3. While the potatoes bake, In a skillet over medium heat, brown the ground meat, tossing often.
4. Put aside to cool. Eliminating surplus fat from the pan involves deglazing its.
5.
6. Add Aromatics: To the skillet with the cooked meat, add the minced garlic and diced onions. Sauté the onions for a few minutes, or until they are transparent and tender.
7. Add BBQ Sauce: Toss in the barbecue sauce, stirring to coat the meat mixture completely. Add salt and pepper to taste. Short-term simmering blends tastes.
8. Tenderize and roast potatoes before slicing. Cool gently after removing from oven. Slicing potatoes lengthwise along their centers should not cut through.
9. Use a fork to fluff the potato before stuffing. Fill each potato to the top with BBQ pork mixture.
10. Shred cheddar cheese and drizzle it over the packed potatoes.
11. Broil: Place stuffed potatoes under the broiler for a few minutes until cheese melts.
12. If desired, top packed potatoes with chopped green onions after baking. If desired, serve warm with sour cream.

NOTE:

➢ You can alter the filling by using your preferred components, like chopped bell peppers, black beans, or corn kernels.

➢ To ensure equal cooking, make sure you select large russet potatoes with similar sizes.

➢ These stuffed potatoes with BBQ beef can be served as a side dish with grilled veggies or as a substantial dinner on their own. Enjoy yourself!

54. HONEY SRIRACHA BBQ WINGS

INGREDIENTS:

- ❖ 2 lbs chicken wings
- ❖ Salt and pepper to taste
- ❖ 1/2 cup honey
- ❖ 1/4 cup Sriracha sauce
- ❖ 1/4 cup barbecue sauce
- ❖ 2 tablespoons soy sauce
- ❖ 2 tablespoons rice vinegar
- ❖ 2 cloves garlic, minced
- ❖ 1 teaspoon grated ginger
- ❖ sesame seeds and chopped green onions (optional garnish)

INSTRUCTIONS:

1. Poven repair: Preheat to 400°F; 200°C.
2. Gently pat chicken wings dry using paper towels. Season with salt and pepper.
3. For seasoned chicken wings, wrap or paper a baking sheet. The wings should be crispy and golden brown after 40–45 minutes in the preheated oven, flipping halfway.
4. Mix honey, rice vinegar, Sriracha, barbecue, soy, minced garlic, and grated ginger in a skillet over medium heat. Mix well and boil. Simmer, stirring periodically, for 5–7 minutes to thicken sauce.
5. Coat Wings: Place chicken wings in a big basin after baking. Coat wings evenly in honey Sriracha BBQ sauce.
6. If preferred, garnish coated wings on a dish with chopped green onions and sesame seeds. Savor and serve hot!

NOTE:

➢ Adjust Sriracha sauce quantity for desired heat. Adjust the amount to your liking.
➢ For extra-crisp wings, broil them for a few minutes after baking.
➢ These Honey Sriracha BBQ Wings are perfect for game days, parties, and other events when you want to wow with spicy, sweet chicken wings. Have fun!

INGREDIENTS:

- ❖ 2 lbs boneless and amskinless chicken breasts or thighs
- ❖ Salt and pepper to taste
- ❖ 1 cup barbecue sauce
- ❖ 1/2 cup chicken broth
- ❖ 1 tablespoon olive oil
- ❖ 1 onion, finely diced
- ❖ 2 cloves garlic, minced
- ❖ 1 teaspoon chili powder
- ❖ 1/2 teaspoon paprika
- ❖ 1/2 teaspoon cumin
- ❖ 1/4 teaspoon cayenne pepper (optional, for extra heat)
- ❖ 8-10 small flour or corn tortillas
- ❖ Toppings: shredded lettuce, diced tomatoes, diced avocado, sliced jalapenos, chopped cilantro, lime wedges, sour cream

INSTRUCTIONS:

1. To prepare the chicken, sprinkle salt and pepper on both sides of the breasts or thighs.

2. To sear the chicken, place a skillet over medium-high heat with olive oil. After adding the chicken, fry it for two to three minutes on each side, or until browned. Remove chicken from skillet and set aside.

3. Sauté aromatics with chopped onion and minced garlic in the same skillet. Sauté onions till fragrant and translucent, 2–3 minutes.Make Sauce: If preferred, add barbecue sauce, chicken broth, paprika, cumin, chili powder, and cayenne pepper to the skillet. Combine everything.

4. Cook Chicken: Nestle the cooked chicken back into the sauce in the skillet. After bringing the sauce to a simmer, turn down the heat. Cook the chicken covered for twenty to twenty-five minutes, or until it is cooked through and soft enough to shred.

5. Shred Chicken: As soon as the chicken is cooked, immediately shred it in the skillet with two forks, thoroughly combining it with the sauce.

6. To assemble the tacos, preheat the tortillas in a microwave or dry skillet. Transfer the pulled chicken with BBQ sauce onto a tortilla.

7. Add Toppings: Sprinkle chopped cilantro, diced tomatoes, diced avocado, sliced jalapenos, diced lettuce, and lime juice on top of the tacos. If preferred, top with a dollop of sour cream.

8. Serve: Enjoy the mouthwatering flavors of the BBQ pulled chicken tacos by serving them right away!

NOTE:

- ➢ Feel free to alter the toppings to suit your tastes. Additional choices consist of coleslaw, salsa, pickled onions, and shredded cheese.
- ➢ Slow-cooker chicken is also possible. Cook all ingredients in the slow cooker on low for 6–8 hours or high for 3–4 hours to soften the chicken enough to shred.BBQ-sauced pulled chicken tacos are ideal for parties or weeknights. Have fun!

56. SMOKED BBQ BAKED BEAN

INGREDIENT:

- ❖ 4 15-ounce cans of your favorite navy, pinto, or black beans
- ❖ drained and rinsed
- ❖ 1/2 lb bacon, diced
- ❖ 1 onion, finely diced
- ❖ 1 bell pepper, finely diced
- ❖ 3 cloves garlic, minced
- ❖ 1 cup barbecue sauce
- ❖ 1/4 cup ketchup
- ❖ 1/4 cup brown sugar
- ❖ 2 tablespoons apple cider vinegar
- ❖ 1 tablespoon Dijon mustard
- ❖ 1 teaspoon Worcestershire sauce
- ❖ Salt and pepper to taste

- ❖ Optional toppings: chopped fresh parsley, green onions, or crispy fried onions

INSTRUCTIONS:

1. To prepare the smoker, preheat it to 250°F, or 120°C. For smoking, use wood chunks or chips of your choosing (applewood, mesquite, or hickory work nicely).
2. Cook diced bacon in a large pan or Render fat in Dutch oven over medium heat for 5 minutes.
3. Prepare the Barbecue Sauce: In a another bowl, thoroughly whisk together Worcestershire sauce, ketchup, brown sugar, apple cider vinegar, Dijon mustard, and barbecue sauce.
4. Toss the beans with the barbecue sauce mixture until evenly coated. Add salt and pepper to taste.
5. Curried Beans: Spoon the bean mixture into a skillet that can be used in the smoker or a throw-away aluminum foil pan. Add the skillet or pan to the smoker that has been warmed.
6. For added flavor, smoke the beans uncovered for two to three hours, stirring from time to time, until the aromas combine and the beans become soft. If burnt beans look dry, cover the pan or skillet with aluminum foil.
7. Serve: Take the smoked BBQ baked beans out of the smoker after they reach the consistency you like. If preferred, add crispy fried onions, green onions, or chopped fresh parsley as a garnish. As a tasty accompaniment to your preferred barbecued meats, serve hot.

NOTE:

➢ Feel free to alter the recipe by substituting chopped jalapenos for more spice, maple syrup for sweetness, or molasses for flavor depth.

➢ Baked beans with leftover smokey barbecue can be kept in the fridge for up to three to four days when kept in an airtight container.Serve them after a brief microwave or stovetop reheat.

➢ For potluck meals, picnics, and get-togethers in the backyard, these smoked BBQ baked beans are ideal. Savor these tasty beans' robust, smokey flavor and texture!

57. BBQ CHICKEN COBB SALAD

INGREDIENTS:

- ❖ 2 boneless, skinless chicken breasts
- ❖ Salt and pepper to taste
- ❖ 1 cup barbecue sauce
- ❖ 6 cups mixed salad greens (romaine, spinach, arugula)
- ❖ 1 cup halved cherry tomatoes
- ❖ 1 large avocado, diced
- ❖ 4 hard-boiled eggs, sliced
- ❖ 1/2 cup crumbled feta or blue
- ❖ 4 slices bacon, cooked and crumbled
- ❖ 1/4 cup thinly sliced red onion
- ❖ Ranch dressing or your favorite dressing for serving

INSTRUCTIONS:

1. Preparing the Chicken: Before cooking the chicken breasts, season them with salt and pepper. Marinate the chicken breasts in a skillet or grill pan over medium-high heat for 6 to 8 minutes per side, or until cooked through. Brush the chicken breasts with barbecue sauce and allow it to caramelize slightly in the last few minutes of cooking. Wait a few minutes after cooking the chicken before cutting it into bite-sized pieces.

2. Salad Preparation: Put the mixed salad greens in a big bowl or onto separate plates. Lay out the toppings in a visually pleasing pattern on top of the greens. You can use diced avocado, hard-boiled egg slices, crumbled blue cheese or feta cheese, crumbled bacon, and thinly sliced red onion.

3. When ready to serve, top the BBQ Chicken Cobb Salad with ranch dressing (or any dressing of your choice), or keep the dressing on the side. Gently mix the salad

INGREDIENTS BY TOSSING IT, AND SAVOR!

NOTE:

➤ Please feel free to add sliced cucumbers, corn kernels, black beans, or toasted nuts to the salad as you choose.

➤ To save time, you can make this salad using leftover grilled or rotisserie chicken.

➤ This BBQ Chicken Cobb Salad is perfect for a light and flavorful lunch or dinner, packed with protein and fresh veggies. Enjoy the combination of smoky barbecue chicken with the classic Cobb salad ingredients!

58. GRILLED BBQ BACON WRAPPED STUFFED JALAPENOS

INGREDIENTS:

- ❖ 12 large jalapeno peppers
- ❖ 8 ounces cream cheese, softened
- ❖ 1 cup shredded cheddar cheese
- ❖ 1 teaspoon garlic powder
- ❖ 1 teaspoon onion powder
- ❖ 1/2 teaspoon smoked paprika
- ❖ Salt and pepper to taste
- ❖ 12 slices bacon
- ❖ 1/2 cup barbecue sauce
- ❖ Toothpicks

INSTRUCTIONS:

1. Grill Prep: Set your grill's temperature to medium-high, between 375 and 400 degrees Fahrenheit.
2. The jalapenos should be halved lengthwise and their seeds and membranes should be spooned out before preparation. Wear gloves to protect your hands from the heated oils.
3. Prepare the Filling: Put melted cream cheese, shredded cheddar cheese, smoked paprika, onion and garlic powders, salt, and pepper in a mixing bowl. Blend until thoroughly blended.
4. Pack the jalapeño halves: Using a spoon, evenly fill each jalapeño half with the cream cheese mixture.
5. Wrap with Bacon: Using a toothpick, wrap a slice of bacon around each packed jalapeño half.
6. Grill: Arrange the stuffed jalapenos wrapped in bacon on the prepared grill. After 15–20 minutes of grilling, turning once, the bacon should be crispy and the peppers should be tender.
7. Brush the jalapeño poppers with barbecue sauce during the final few minutes of grilling so that it may slightly caramelize.
8. Serve: Take the stuffed jalapenos from the grill and place them on a serving plate after the bacon is crispy and cooked through. Enjoy while hot!

NOTE:

➢ You can change the jalapeño poppers' level of heat by removing all of the seeds and membranes for a mellower taste, or keeping some of them intact for more spiciness.

➢ To keep the toothpicks from burning on the grill, soak them in water for around half an hour before usage.

➢ When serving as an appetizer at BBQ parties, game days, or any other event where you want to wow your guests with a flavorful and hot dish, these Grilled BBQ Bacon Wrapped Stuffed Jalapenos are ideal!

59. BBQ PULLED PORK STUFFED BELL PEPPERS

INGREDIENT:

- ❖ Four huge bell peppers of any color, peeled and cut in half
- ❖ 2 cups cooked pulled pork (homemade or store-bought)
- ❖ 1 cup cooked quinoa or rice
- ❖ 1/2 cup barbecue sauce
- ❖ 1/2 cup shredded cheddar cheese
- ❖ 2 green onions, thinly sliced
- ❖ Salt and pepper to taste
- ❖ Optional toppings: chopped fresh cilantro, diced avocado, sour cream

INSTRUCTIONS:

1. Oven Prep: Set the oven's temperature to 375°F, or 190°C.
2. Cut the bell peppers lengthwise, then scoop off the seeds and membranes to get them ready.Place pepper halves cut-side up on a baking sheet.
3. Prepare Filling: In a large mixing dish, combine pulled pork, rice or quinoa, shredded cheddar cheese, barbecue sauce, and chopped green onions.Adjust salt and pepper to taste. Stir in all ingredients.
4. Bell Pepper Stuffing: Evenly spoon the pulled pork mixture into each half of a bell pepper, gently pressing to pack the filling.
5. Bake: Bake the bell peppers for 25 to 30 minutes, or until they are soft, in a preheated oven, covered with aluminum foil.
6. Not required Serving and Topping: Take off the foil from the baking dish and top the stuffed bell peppers with diced avocado, fresh cilantro, and, if you'd like, a dollop of sour cream. Enjoy while hot!

NOTE:

➢ Feel free to use additional ingredients, such as diced tomatoes, diced onions, black beans, or corn, to customize the filling.
➢ For this dish, you may repurpose leftover pulled pork or make it from scratch using your preferred technique (such as an Instant Pot or slow cooker).

➤ These tasty and filling BBQ Pulled Pork Stuffed Bell Peppers are the ideal dish. For a full supper, serve them with a coleslaw or side salad. Have fun!

60. CAJUN BBQ SHRIMP

INGREDIENTS:

- ❖ 1 lb large shrimp, peeled and deveined
- ❖ 2 tablespoons Cajun seasoning
- ❖ 2 tablespoons olive oil
- ❖ 4 cloves garlic, minced
- ❖ 1/4 cup barbecue sauce
- ❖ 2 tablespoons Worcestershire sauce
- ❖ 2 tablespoons lemon juice
- ❖ 2 tablespoons chopped fresh parsley
- ❖ Salt and pepper to taste
- ❖ Lemon wedges for serving
- ❖ Cooked rice or crusty bread for serving

INSTRUCTIONS:

1. To prepare the shrimp for marinating, peel and devein them. Then, bring a bowl to a boil and add the shrimp, garlic, salt, pepper, and Cajun seasoning. Stir to coat. Toss the shrimp around in the spice blend to cover them evenly. Put the shrimp in the fridge for 15 to 30 minutes to marinate so the flavors can combine.

2. Cleaning the Grill or Skillet: Preheat your grill to medium-high, or around 375 to 400 degrees Fahrenheit. Another option is to use a large skillet set over medium-high heat on the stovetop.

3. How to Cook Shrimp: For grilling, thread shrimp that have been marinated onto skewers. The shrimp need to be cooked for two or three minutes per side, or until they are opaque pink and have beautiful grill marks. To cook the shrimp, heat some olive oil in a skillet and sauté the shrimp for a couple of minutes per side, or until they are opaque throughout.

4. Worcestershire sauce, lemon juice, and barbecue sauce are all mixed together in a small saucepan to make the BBQ sauce. Simmer, stirring periodically, for five to seven minutes after the sauce has thickened. Put the pot off the heat.

5. Coat Shrimp: Evenly coat the grilled or cooked shrimp by brushing them with the prepared BBQ sauce. Alternatively, you might put the shrimp in a bowl and toss them in the sauce.

6. on serve, move the Cajun BBQ shrimp on a dish and top with freshly cut parsley. Serve hot, with wedges of lemon available to squeeze over the shrimp. In order to let the

crispy bread soak up the rich sauce, you can also serve the shrimp over cooked rice.

NOTE:

- ➢ Vary the amount of Cajun seasoning to suit your level of heat tolerance. To fit your preferences, you can change the amount.
- ➢ If you want more heat, feel free to add more Cajun spices or spicy sauce.
- ➢ Serve these Cajun BBQ Shrimp as a main course with your preferred sides, or as an appetizer with toothpicks for convenient snacking. Savor the robust and piquant tastes of this mouthwatering shrimp dish!

61. BBQ PORK RAMEN

INGREDIENTS:

- ❖ 8 oz ramen noodles (fresh or dried)
- ❖ 1 lb BBQ pork (either leftover or store-bought)
- ❖ 6 cups chicken or vegetable broth
- ❖ 2 tablespoons soy sauce
- ❖ 2 tablespoons hoisin sauce
- ❖ 1 tablespoon sesame oil
- ❖ 4 cloves garlic, minced
- ❖ 1 tablespoon fresh ginger, grated
- ❖ 2 sliced green onions (white and green sections separated)
- ❖ 2 cups baby spinach or bok choy, chopped
- ❖ 2 soft-boiled eggs, peeled and halved (optional)
- ❖ Toasted sesame seeds for garnish (optional)
- ❖ Sriracha or chili oil for serving (optional)

INSTRUCTIONS:

1. Prepare the Ramen Noodles: Follow the directions on the package to cook the ramen noodles. After cooking, reserve and drain.

2. Prepare the BBQ Pork: If the pork isn't cooked through, reheat it in a skillet or microwave. Cut the pork into small pieces using a knife or shred it, then set it aside.

3. To make the broth, place a large saucepan over medium heat with the sesame oil. Add the white portions of the cut green onions, minced garlic, and grated ginger. Sauté until aromatic, one to two minutes.

4. Add the seasonings and broth. Add the broth, either vegetable or chicken. AAdd the soy sauce and hoisin sauce and mix well. To let the flavors combine, boil the broth for about five minutes over low heat.

5. Prepare ramen bowls: Transfer cooked noodles to separate plates and top with a spoon. Ladle the hot broth over the noodles.

6. Add Toppings: Top the ramen bowls with the sliced or shredded BBQ pork, chopped bok choy or baby spinach, and soft-boiled eggs, if using.

7. Garnish and Serve: Add toasted sesame seeds and the green sections of sliced green onions to the BBQ pork ramen. If preferred, serve hot with extra spice from Sriracha or chili oil on the side.

NOTE:

➤ Feel free to alter the toppings to suit your tastes. Nori strips, corn kernels, bamboo shoots, and sliced mushrooms are more alternatives.

➤ Tofu or tempeh can be used in place of the BBQ pork in a vegetarian version, and vegetable broth can be used in place of chicken stock.

➤ A tasty and soothing dish that's ideal for a quiet night in is BBQ Pork Ramen. Savor the flavorful soup, succulent BBQ pork, and succulent noodles!

62. SMOKED BBQ CHICKEN THIGHS

INGREDIENTS:

- ❖ 8 bone-in, skin-on chicken thighs
- ❖ Salt and pepper to taste
- ❖ 1 cup barbecue sauce (store-bought or homemade)
- ❖ 2 tablespoons olive oil
- ❖ 2 teaspoons smoked paprika
- ❖ 1 teaspoon garlic powder
- ❖ 1 teaspoon onion powder
- ❖ 1/2 teaspoon cayenne pepper (optional, for extra heat)
- ❖ Optimal garnishes include freshly chopped parsley or green onions.

INSTRUCTION:

1. Prepare the Chicken Thighs: Using paper towels, pat dry the chicken thighs to absorb any extra moisture. Give them a liberal amount of salt and pepper on both sides.

2. Make the BBQ Rub: In a small bowl, combine the olive oil, onion, garlic, and smoked paprika powders, as well as the cayenne pepper, if using.

3. Garnish Chicken Thighs: Make sure the seasoned chicken thighs are evenly covered with BBQ rub by giving them a thorough rubdown.

4. Heat up the smoker: Set your smoker's temperature to 250°F (120°C) and add your preferred wood chips or chunks (applewood, hickory, mesquite, etc.).

5. Put seasoned chicken thighs skin-side up on the grates when the smoker is hot. Smoke for one hour or until done. Give it a crispy, golden brown outside and smoke it for 2–2 1/2 hoursuntil the interior reaches 165°F, or 75°C.

6. Brush barbecue sauce evenly on chicken thighs in the last 30 minutes of smoking to glaze them.Flip the chicken thighs after 10–15 minutes and cook for 5–10 minutes until done and sauced.

7. After the chicken thighs are cooked, take them out of the smoker and give them some time to rest before serving. If desired, add some freshly chopped parsley or green onions as a garnish. The delicious, smoky BBQ chicken thighs are best served hot.

NOTE:

➢ It is essential to keep an eye on the smoker's temperature so that the cooking temperature remains constant.

➢ A meat thermometer can be used to assess the doneness of the chicken thighs by measuring their interior temperature.

➢ These tasty and tender Smoked BBQ Chicken Thighs are the ideal dish to serve at picnics and backyard barbecues, or any other occasion where you want to wow guests. Savor the juicy, delicate flesh and the enticing smokey scent!

63. BBQ TOFU LETTUCE WRAPS

INGREDIENTS:

- ❖ 1 block extra-firm tofu, pressed and drained
- ❖ 1/2 cup barbecue sauce (store-bought or homemade)
- ❖ 2 tablespoons soy sauce or tamari
- ❖ 1 tablespoon maple syrup or agave nectar
- ❖ 1 tablespoon olive oil
- ❖ 1 teaspoon smoked paprika
- ❖ 1 teaspoon garlic powder
- ❖ 1 teaspoon onion powder
- ❖ 1/2 teaspoon ground cumin
- ❖ Salt and pepper to taste
- ❖ 1 tablespoon sesame seeds (optional, for garnish)
- ❖ Leaves taken from one head of butter lettuce or romaine lettuce
- ❖ Optional toppings: shredded carrots, sliced cucumber, diced avocado, sliced green onions, chopped cilantro

INSTRUCTIONS:

1. Tofu preparation: Set oven temperature to 400°F (200°C). Slice the drained and pressed tofu into thin strips or cubes.

2. Prepare the Barbecue Marinade: Combine barbecue sauce, agave nectar or maple syrup, tamari or soy sauce, olive oil, smoked paprika, ground cumin, onion powder and garlic powder, and salt & pepper in a bowl and whisk until thoroughly blended.

3. Tofu should be marinated. Tofu cubes or strips should be put in a shallow dish or plastic bag that can be sealed. After pouring the BBQ marinade over the tofu, toss to ensure even coating. Give the tofu a minimum of 15 to 30 minutes to marinade, or longer for maximum flavor.

4. To bake the tofu, lightly oil or line a baking sheet with parchment paper. On the baking sheet, arrange the marinated tofu in a single layer. Bake the tofu, flipping halfway through, until crisp and golden, at 200 degrees Fahrenheit.

5. To assemble the lettuce wraps, put a dollop of barbecued tofu on top of each leaf of lettuce. If preferred, garnish with chopped cilantro, sesame seeds, diced avocado, sliced green onions, sliced cucumber, and shredded carrots.

6. Serve: As a light and refreshing dinner or appetizer, serve the BBQ Tofu Lettuce Wraps right away. Savor the mouthwatering textures and flavors!

NOTE:

➢ Feel free to add more ingredients like lime juice, chili flakes, or ginger for taste, or to customize the BBQ tofu marinade with your favorite flavors.

➢ Other lettuce leaves or wraps, like iceberg lettuce, cabbage leaves, or collard greens, can also be used.

➢ this flavorful and simple vegan lunch ideas, such as this BBQ Tofu Lettuce Wraps, are loaded with protein. Savor the contrast of crisp, fresh vegetables and smokey BBQ tofu enclosed in soft lettuce leaves!

64. KOREAN BBQ CHICKEN WINGS

INGREDIENTS:

- ❖ 2 lbs chicken wings, separated into drumettes and flats
- ❖ Salt and pepper to taste
- ❖ 1/4 cup soy sauce
- ❖ 2 tablespoons brown sugar
- ❖ 2 tablespoons rice vinegar
- ❖ 2 tablespoons sesame oil
- ❖ 2 cloves garlic, minced
- ❖ 1 teaspoon grated ginger
- ❖ 1 tablespoon gochujang (Korean chili paste)
- ❖ 1 tablespoon honey or maple syrup
- ❖ 2 green onions, thinly sliced (for garnish)
- ❖ Toasted sesame seeds (for garnish)

INSTRUCTIONS:

1. Dry the chicken wings by patting them with paper towels to remove any extra moisture. Flavor them with salt and pepper according to your preference.

2. Make a marinade for Korean BBQ: In a mixing bowl, combine the following ingredients: rice vinegar, soy sauce, brown sugar, gochujang, black garlic, shredded ginger, sesame oil, and honey or maple syrup. To ensure a smooth mixture, whisk all of the components together.

3. Prepare chicken wings by soaking them in a marinade. Position the chicken wings into a spacious hermetically sealed plastic bag or a flat container. Drizzle the Korean

4. BBQ marinade onto the chicken wings, ensuring that they are thoroughly and evenly covered.To allow the flavors to seep in, refrigerate the marinated mixture for at least an hour or, better yet, overnight.

5. Grill Preheating: Set your grill to medium-high heat, specifically between 375°F and 400°F.

6. Grill Chicken Wings: Take out the chicken wings from the marinade and get rid of any extra marinade. Position the wings onto the prepared grill and grill for 15-20 minutes, rotating periodically, until they are fully cooked and have a desirable charred appearance on all surfaces.

7. Decorate and Present: Relocate the grilled Korean BBQ chicken wings to a dish intended for serving. Decorate with finely cut green onions and toasted sesame seeds. Heat the dish and savor the delicious tastes!

NOTE:

➢ Please be aware that an alternative option is available for cooking the marinated chicken wings. You have the choice to utilize the oven by baking them at a temperature of 400°F (200°C) for a duration of 25-30 minutes until they are fully cooked and have a crispy texture.

➢ Modify the quantity of gochujang based on your preferred degree of spiciness. You have the option to adjust the quantity to your preference, either by increasing or decreasing it.

➢ The Korean BBQ Chicken Wings are ideal for serving as an appetizer, party snack, or main dish over steamed rice and vegetables. Indulge in the robust and delectable flavors of this mouthwatering Korean-inspired cuisine!

65. BBQ CHICKEN AND PINEAPPLE SKEWERS

INGREDIENT:

- ❖ One pound of skinless, boneless chicken thighs or breasts, chopped into bite-sized pieces
- ❖ One small pineapple that has been cored, peeled, and sliced
- ❖ One bell pepper, chopped into bits, any color
- ❖ One red onion, sliced into pieces
- ❖ Metal or wood skewers; if wood, soak the skewers in water for half an hour before using.
- ❖ To taste, add salt and pepper.
- ❖ Barbecue sauce for serving and basting
- ❖ Fresh parsley or cilantro, chopped (optional)

INSTRUCTIONS:

1. Prepare Chicken and Pineapple: Season the chicken pieces with an appropriate amount of salt and pepper. Skewer the chicken, pineapple chunks, bell pepper pieces, and red onion chunks by threading them onto skewers in an alternating pattern.

2. Grill Preheating: Set your grill to a medium-high temperature, specifically between 375°F and 400°F.

3. Grill Skewers: Position the constructed skewers on the heating grill. Prepare the dish by cooking it for a duration of 8-10 minutes, ensuring to stir it periodically. This will result in fully cooked chicken and soft veggies with a small scorched appearance.

4. Brush BBQ sauce on skewers at the conclusion of grilling. Turn the skewers occasionally and add sauce to both sides until the chicken and vegetables are evenly covered and slightly browned.

5. Serve: After thoroughly cooking the BBQ Chicken and Pineapple Skewers and coating them with BBQ sauce, take them off the grill and place them on a tray for serving. If preferred, add a garnish of finely chopped fresh cilantro or parsley. Present the dish while it is still hot, and provide additional BBQ sauce on the side for dipping or drizzling.

NOTE:

➤ Please feel at liberty to personalize the skewers by adding extra vegetables such as cherry tomatoes, zucchini, or mushrooms.

➤ You have the option to utilize commercially available BBQ sauce or create your own homemade BBQ sauce for the purpose of basting and serving.

➤ These BBQ Chicken and Pineapple Skewers are ideal for summer BBQs, picnics, or any outdoor occasion. Indulge in the delectable combination of grilled chicken, pineapple, and vegetables, which offers a delightful blend of sweet and savory flavors.

INGREDIENTS:

- ❖ 4 medium zucchini
- ❖ 2 cups cooked shredded chicken (rotisserie works)
- ❖ 1/2 cup barbecue sauce
- ❖ 1/2 cup shredded mozzarella cheese
- ❖ 1/3 cups diced red onion
- ❖ 1/3 cups diced bell pepper (any color)
- ❖ 2 cloves garlic, minced
- ❖ 2 tablespoons olive oil
- ❖ Salt and pepper to taste
- ❖ Optional chopped fresh parsley or cilantro garnish

INSTRUCTIONS:

1. Preheat Oven: Set your oven to a temperature of 400°F (200°C) before using it.

2. Prepare Zucchini: Slice each zucchini in half vertically. Utilize a spoon to extract the seeds and establish a vacant core, therefore fashioning "boats."

3. Prepare Filling: In a spacious mixing bowl, mix together the cooked shredded chicken, barbecue sauce, shredded mozzarella cheese, sliced red onion, diced bell pepper, minced garlic, olive oil, salt, and pepper. Blend until all elements are thoroughly incorporated.

4. Zucchini Boats: Place the excavated zucchini halves on a parchment- or aluminum-foil-lined baking sheet Apply mild pressure to pack the BBQ chicken filling evenly into the zucchini boats.

5. Bake: For 20 to 25 minutes, or when

6. the stew is hot and bubbling and the zucchini is tender, bake the baking sheet in a preheated oven.

7. After cooking the BBQ Chicken Stuffed Zucchini Boats, take them out of the oven. If preferred, add a garnish of finely chopped fresh parsley or cilantro. Heat and savor!

NOTE:

➤ Please feel at liberty to personalize the filling by incorporating supplementary ingredients like as diced tomatoes, corn kernels, black beans, or jalapenos to enhance the taste and texture.

➤ Prior to baking, you may optionally evenly distribute additional shredded cheese on the surface of the packed zucchini boats to achieve a more indulgent and cheesy outcome.

➤ These BBQ Chicken Stuffed Zucchini Boats are a delectable and healthful dish, ideal for a quick weekday dinner or a flavorful snack for social events. Indulge in the delectable blend of delicate zucchini and savory BBQ chicken stuffing!

67. GRILLED BBQ CHICKEN BURRITOS

INGREDIENT:

- ❖ Chicken breasts or thighs, without bones and skin, weighing 1 pound
- ❖ Salt and pepper to taste
- ❖ 1 cup barbecue sauce
- ❖ 1 tablespoon olive oil
- ❖ 1 onion, diced
- ❖ 1 bell pepper (any color), diced
- ❖ 1 cup cooked rice
- ❖ 1 cup drained, rinsed canned black beans
- ❖ One
- ❖ cup shredded cheddar or Mexican cheese blend
- ❖ 4 large flour tortillas
- ❖ Optional toppings: diced tomatoes, sliced avocado, shredded lettuce, sour cream, salsa, chopped cilantro

INSTRUCTIONS:

1. Prepare Chicken: Salt and pepper chicken breasts or thighs to taste. BBQ sauce both sides of the chicken, storing the rest for later.

2. To grill chicken, heat your grill to 375°F–400°F. Grill the chicken until fully cooked and blackened, 6-8 minutes per side. Once off the grill, let the item rest before cutting it into strips or cubes.

3. Sauté vegetables: Medium-heat olive oil in a skillet. Sauté the diced onion and bell pepper for 5-7 minutes until soft.

4. Prepare burritos: Lay wheat tortillas flat. Spread cooked rice, black beans, grilled BBQ chicken strips, sautéed veggies, and shredded cheese on tortillas.

5. Fold each tortilla's sides inward and tightly roll them to make burritos.

6. Heat your grill to medium for burritos. Place folded burritos on grill grates with the folded side down. Grill tortillas for 2-3 minutes per side until golden brown and crispy.

7. Serve: Transfer grilled BBQ chicken burritos to a serving tray. Cover with remaining barbecue sauce and serve with diced tomatoes, avocado, lettuce, sour cream, salsa, and cilantro.

NOTE:

➢ Please feel at liberty to personalize the burritos by adding extra fillings such as corn kernels, diced jalapenos, or sliced olives.

➢ For a more expedient preparation, you may opt to utilize pre-cooked chicken, such as leftover cooked chicken or rotisserie chicken, as an alternative to grilling chicken breasts or thighs.

➢ These Grilled BBQ Chicken Burritos are ideal for a delectable and fulfilling meal that is suitable for both lunch and dinner. Indulge in the savory BBQ essence enveloped in toasted and crunchy tortillas!

68. BBQ BACON WRAPPED BRUSSELS SPROUTS

INGREDIENTS:

- ❖ 1 lb Brussels sprouts, trimmed and halved
- ❖ 8 slices bacon, cut in half crosswise
- ❖ 1/4 cup barbecue sauce
- ❖ Toothpicks

INSTRUCTIONS:

1. Preheat Oven: Set your oven to a temperature of 400°F (200°C) before using it. If you want to clean your baking sheet easier, line it with parchment paper or aluminum foil.
2. After peeling the stiff outer layers, cut Brussels sprouts in half lengthwise.

3. Start by halving Brussels sprouts. Wrap each sprout with half a bacon piece. To secure the bacon, stick a toothpick into the Brussels sprout and bacon simultaneously.
4. Place Brussels sprouts on a baking pan and cover with BBQ sauce and bacon. First coat each one evenly with barbecue sauce, then generously apply.
5. Before putting the baking sheet in the prepared oven, fry the bacon and sprouts for 25–30 minutes until tender and golden. Flip the contents halfway through baking for even cooking.
6. Prepare: BBQ Bacon Once the Brussels sprouts are fully cooked and have become crispy, take them out of the oven and allow them to cool down a bit. Present the meal at a high temperature as a delectable starter or accompaniment.

NOTE:

➢ Please be aware that you have the option to personalize the taste by utilizing several kinds of barbecue sauce, such as those with a sweet and smoky, spicy, or tangy flavor profile.
➢ If desired, you have the option to prepare these BBQ Bacon Wrapped Brussels Sprouts on the grill as an alternative to baking them in the oven. To cook the bacon-wrapped Brussels sprouts, first preheat your grill to medium-high heat. Then, grill the sprouts for 10-15 minutes, making sure to turn them occasionally. Keep

grilling until the bacon becomes crispy and the Brussels sprouts become tender.

➢ These BBQ Bacon Wrapped Brussels Sprouts are ideal for social events, celebrations, or as a delectable appetizer. Indulge in the irresistible fusion of savory bacon, delectably sweet barbecue sauce, and delicate Brussels sprouts!

69. HONEY GARLIC BBQ CHICKEN

INGREDIENTS:

- ❖ 4 boneless, skinless chicken breasts
- ❖ 1/2 cup BBQ sauce
- ❖ 1/4 cup honey
- ❖ 3 cloves garlic, minced
- ❖ 2 tablespoons soy sauce
- ❖ 1 tablespoon olive oil
- ❖ Salt and pepper to taste
- ❖ Chopped parsley for garnish (optional)

INSTRUCTIONS:

1. Combine the following ingredients in a small bowl: honey, soy sauce, olive oil, minced garlic, BBQ sauce, salt, and pepper.
2. Marinate chicken breasts equally in a shallow dish or plastic bag. To optimize taste, refrigerate the dish for an hour or overnight.
3. Before you start cooking, get the grill up to a medium-high heat. Take the chicken out of the marinade, shaking off any excess marinade, and set aside the rest.
4. Chicken breasts should be 165 degrees Fahrenheit (75 degrees Celsius) and juices clear after 6–7 minutes per side on the grill.
5. After the chicken is cooked, take it off the grill and allow it to rest for a few period before cutting it into slices.
6. Optionally, adorn with finely diced parsley and serve while still warm.

NOTE:

➢ Please note that if you desire a more sweet taste, you have the option to augment the quantity of honey in the marinade. Alternatively, if you desire a more acidic flavor, you can incorporate a little amount of apple cider vinegar or lemon juice. This adaptable dish is compatible with alternative protein sources like as pork chops or even tofu, making it suitable for vegetarians. Modify the grilling duration appropriately, taking into account the thickness of the protein you have selected. Savor the delectable Honey Garlic BBQ Chicken.

70. SMOKED BBQ MEATBALLS

INGREDIENTS:

- ❖ 1 lb ground beef
- ❖ 1/2 cup breadcrumbs
- ❖ 1/4 cup grated Parmesan cheese
- ❖ 1/4 cup finely chopped onion
- ❖ 2 cloves garlic, minced
- ❖ 1 egg, beaten
- ❖ 1/4 cup milk
- ❖ 1 teaspoon Worcestershire sauce
- ❖ 1/2 teaspoon salt
- ❖ 1/4 teaspoon black pepper
- ❖ 1 cup BBQ sauce
- ❖ 2 tablespoons honey
- ❖ 1 tablespoon apple cider vinegar
- ❖ 1 teaspoon smoked paprika
- ❖ 1/2 teaspoon chili powder
- ❖ Chopped parsley for garnish (optional)

INSTRUCTIONS:

1. As suggested by the manufacturer, heat your smoker to 225°F (110°C) and choose your wood chips for smoking flavor.

2. Toss together the ground beef, breadcrumbs, Parmesan cheese, chopped onion, minced garlic, beaten egg, milk, Worcestershire sauce, salt, and black pepper in a big serving bowl. Be sure to mix thoroughly.

3. Form the mixture into meatballs, approximately 1 inch in diameter, and position them on a wire rack.

4. Position the wire rack containing the meatballs inside the smoker. Cover the cover tightly and smoke the meatballs for a duration of 1.5 to 2 hours, or until they are fully cooked and have assimilated a desirable amount of smokey essence.

5. Combine BBQ sauce, honey, apple cider vinegar, smoked paprika, and chili powder in a small pot. Apply heat at a moderate level, stirring regularly, until the sauce reaches a warmed state and becomes slightly thicker.

6. After smoking the meatballs, take them out of the smoker and place them in a spacious bowl. Drizzle the heated BBQ sauce onto the meatballs and delicately mix to ensure even coverage.

7. Transfer the meatballs coated in sauce to a dish for serving. Optionally, garnish with chopped parsley and serve while hot.

NOTE:

➢ To enhance the intensity of smokiness, it is possible to incorporate more wood chips during the midpoint of the smoking procedure. These smoked BBQ meatballs are ideal for serving as an appetizer at gatherings or as a main course accompanied by mashed potatoes and roasted veggies. Additionally, it is possible to prepare a bigger quantity of meatballs and then freeze them after cooking for future consumption. Savor the delectable and flavorful smokiness!

71. SMOKED BBQ MEATBALLS

INGREDIENTS:

- ❖ 1 lb ground beef
- ❖ 1/2 cup breadcrumbs
- ❖ 1/4 cup grated Parmesan cheese
- ❖ 1/4 cup finely chopped onion
- ❖ 2 cloves garlic, minced
- ❖ 1 egg, beaten
- ❖ 1/4 cup milk
- ❖ 1 teaspoon Worcestershire sauce
- ❖ 1/2 teaspoon salt
- ❖ 1/4 teaspoon black pepper
- ❖ 1 cup BBQ sauce
- ❖ 2 tablespoons honey
- ❖ 1 tablespoon apple cider vinegar
- ❖ 1 teaspoon smoked paprika
- ❖ 1/2 teaspoon chili powder
- ❖ Chopped parsley for garnish (optional)

INSTRUCTIONS:

1. As directed by the manufacturer, preheat your smoker to 225°F (110°C) and use your preferred wood chips to add a smokey flavor.

2. Ground beef, breadcrumbs, Parmesan cheese, minced garlic, chopped onion, beaten egg, milk, Worcestershire sauce, salt, and black pepper should all be combined in a big mixing basin. Blend until thoroughly blended.

3. After forming the mixture into meatballs with a diameter of about an inch, arrange them on a wire rack.

4. Put the meatballs on the wire rack and cover it with the smoker. Once the meatballs are thoroughly cooked and have taken on some smokey flavor, cover the container and smoke it for one to two hours.

5. Put the smoked paprika, chili powder, honey, apple cider vinegar, and BBQ sauce in a small pot. Stirring regularly, boil the sauce over medium heat until it thickens slightly and gets warmed through.

6. After the meatballs are done smoking, take them out of the smoker and place them in a big bowl. Drizzle the meatballs with the warm barbecue sauce and toss to coat.

7. Place the meatballs with sauce on a dish, top with chopped parsley if preferred, and serve immediately.

NOTE:

➤ About halfway through the smoking process, add a few additional wood chips for even more smoky flavor. These meatballs with smoked BBQ sauce make a great party appetizer or main course when paired with mashed potatoes and roasted vegetables. Make a bigger quantity and save the cooked meatballs in the freezer for another time. Savor the mouthwatering goodness of smoke!

72. BBQ CHICKEN AND AVOCADO SALAD

INGREDIENTS:

- ❖ 2 boneless, skinless chicken breasts
- ❖ Salt and pepper to taste
- ❖ 1 cup BBQ sauce
- ❖ 6 cups mixed salad greens (such as lettuce, spinach, or arugula)
- ❖ 1 avocado, diced
- ❖ 1 cup cherry tomatoes, halved
- ❖ 1/2 cup corn kernels (fresh and canned, or frozen)
- ❖ 1/4 cup diced red onion
- ❖ 1/4 cup shredded cheddar cheese
- ❖ Optional garnish: chopped fresh cilantro, tortilla strips

For the dressing:

- ❖ 1/4 cup BBQ sauce
- ❖ 2 tablespoons olive oil
- ❖ 1 tablespoon apple cider vinegar
- ❖ 1 teaspoon honey
- ❖ Salt and pepper to taste

INSTRUCTIONS:

1. Pepper and salt both sides of chicken breasts.
2. Heat grill pan or grill to medium-high. Grill chicken breasts 6–7 minutes per side until cooked through and no longer pink from the middle.
3. In the last few minutes
4. of grilling, brush BBQ sauce on both sides to caramelize chicken breasts. Slice the chicken after resting for a few minutes from the grill.
5. To make the dressing, mix apple cider vinegar, honey, olive oil, BBQ sauce, salt, and pepper in a separate bowl. Set aside.
6. Prepare a large salad with chopped avocado, cherry tomatoes, corn kernels, diced red onion, and mixed salad greens.
7. Thinly slice grilled BBQ chicken breasts and add to salad.
8. Cover the salad
9. with dressing and gently mix.
10. Sprinkle shredded cheddar on salad.
11. Add tortilla strips and chopped cilantro if desired.
12. Serve immediately as a hearty, light dinner.

NOTE:

➢ Feel free to add your preferred toppings, like diced cucumber, sliced bell peppers, or black beans, to this salad.

➢ You can substitute grilled tofu or tempeh for the chicken in this recipe if you'd rather make it vegetarian.

➢ This avocado and chicken salad with barbecue sauce makes a quick lunch or dinner, especially in the summer. Savor the smoky BBQ flavors paired with fresh veggies and creamy avocado!

73. GRILLED BBQ PORK TENDERLOIN

INGREDIENTS:

- ❖ 2 pork tenderloins, each weighing around 1 to 1.5 pounds
- ❖ Salt and pepper to taste
- ❖ 1 cup BBQ sauce
- ❖ 2 tablespoons olive oil
- ❖ 2 cloves garlic, minced
- ❖ Garnish with chopped fresh herbs (parsley, cilantro, etc.) if desired.

INSTRUCTIONS:

1. Grill over medium-high heat until the temperature reaches 375–400°F, or 190–200°C.
2. If needed, trim the pork tenderloins of any extra fat or silver skin. To remove stains, gently pat with paper towels.
3. Salt and pepper pork tenderloins generously.

4. Mix BBQ sauce, olive oil, and minced garlic in a small bowl.
5. Mix a little BBQ sauce with the pork tenderloinsand cover well.
6. The pork tenderloins should be grilled for around fifteen to twenty minutes, turning them over halfway through, or until they achieve an internal temperature of 145 degrees Fahrenheit (63 degrees Celsius). Use a meat thermometer to determine when the meat is done cooking.
7. For a little caramelization, brush additional BBQ sauce over the pork tenderloins in the last few minutes of grilling.
8. Once the pork tenderloins are cooked to your liking and have a nice char, take them from the grill and set them on a separate cutting board.
9. Spend a few minutes letting the pork tenderloins rest before slicing them into thick medallions.
10. Serve hot with additional BBQ sauce on the side and sprinkle with finely chopped fresh herbs if desired.

NOTE:

- ➤ o avoid dry pork tenderloins, cook them for just the right amount of time. A USDA-recommended cooking time for pork is 15 to 20 minutes per side, with a 3-minute rest period in between, until the internal temperature reaches 145 to 63 degrees Celsius.
- ➤ If you have more time, you can marinate the pork tenderloins in the BBQ sauce mixture for more flavor, but it's not required.
- ➤ For a tasty and filling supper, serve this Grilled BBQ Pork Tenderloin with your preferred side dishes, including grilled veggies, corn on the cob, or a crisp salad!

74. BBQ CHICKEN FAJITAS

INGREDIENTS:

- ❖ 1 pound of thinly sliced, skinless, boneless chicken breasts
- ❖ 2 bell peppers (any color), sliced
- ❖ 1 onion, sliced
- ❖ 2 tablespoons olive oil
- ❖ 1/4 cup BBQ sauce
- ❖ 2 teaspoons chili powder
- ❖ 1 teaspoon ground cumin
- ❖ 1 teaspoon paprika
- ❖ 1/2 teaspoon garlic powder
- ❖ 1/2 teaspoon onion powder
- ❖ Salt and pepper to taste
- ❖ Flour tortillas
- ❖ Optional toppings: shredded cheese, sour cream, salsa, guacamole, chopped cilantro, lime wedges.

INSTRUCTIONS:

1. In a separate bowl, add pepper, ground cumin, paprika, onion, and garlic powders to make the marinade.
2. Place sliced chicken breast strips in a shallow dish or plastic bag and close. Make sure the chicken is fully covered in marinade. Best taste comes from 30–4 hours
3. of fridge marinating.
4. In a big skillet or grill pan set over medium-high heat, warm up one tablespoon of olive oil. Chop the bell peppers and onions and sauté them in a skillet.
5. Melt the
6. second tablespoon of olive oil in a skillet over medium heat. Remove excess marinade from the chicken breast strips and place in the skillet. Brown and cook the chicken for 6-8 minutes in a simmering pan, turning once halfway through.
7. Put the chicken back in the pan along with the vegetables. Mix all ingredients well and heat until heated through.
8. Heat flour tortillas
9. per package instructions.
10. Serve the BBQ chicken and veggie mixture over warm tortillas.Toss in with chopped cilantro, sour cream, cheese, salsa, guacamole, or lime juice, or any other toppings you choose.
11. After rolling up the tortillas, savor your succulent BBQ chicken fajitas!

NOTE:

➢ Feel free to add more ingredients or toppings to the fajitas, including diced tomatoes, rice, or black beans.

➢ For a smokier taste, you can also grill the chicken and veggies outside.

➢ These easy and quick evening meals, or as an engaging dish for guests at a backyard BBQ, are these BBQ Chicken Fajitas. Have fun!

75. SMOKED BBQ BEEF SHORT RIBS

INGREDIENTS:

- ❖ 4-6 beef short ribs, about 2-3 pounds (bone-in)
- ❖ Salt and black pepper to taste
- ❖ 2 tablespoons olive oil
- ❖ For the dry rub:
- ❖ 2 tablespoons brown sugar
- ❖ 1 tablespoon paprika
- ❖ 1 tablespoon garlic powder
- ❖ 1 tablespoon onion powder
- ❖ 1 tablespoon chili powder
- ❖ 1 teaspoon ground cumin
- ❖ 1 teaspoon ground mustard
- ❖ 1 teaspoon cayenne pepper (adjust to taste)
- ❖ 1 cup BBQ sauce (your favorite store-bought or homemade)

- ❖ Chops or pieces of smoking wood (applewood, hickory, or oak are good options)

INSTRUCTIONS:

1. Start your smoker at 225°F, or 107°C. To make smoke, use wood chunks or chips.
2. All of the dry rub's ingredients—brown sugar, paprika, cayenne pepper, onion, garlic, chile, cumin, ground mustard, and black pepper—should be combined in a small bowl.
3. Make careful to coat both sides of the beef short ribs with a generous amount of dry rub after coating them in olive oil.
4. The seasoned beef short ribs should be placed directly on the smoker racks, bone side down, as soon as the smoker is heated and smoking.
5. Once the internal temperature of the beef short ribs reaches approximately 200°F (93°C) and the meat begins to come away from the bones, cover the smoker and allow the meat to smoke for four to six hours.
6. Brush the short ribs with BBQ sauce during the final hour of smoking, making sure to coat both sides well.
7. When the short ribs are tender and finished smoking, take them out of the smoker and allow them to rest for ten to fifteen minutes before serving.
8. If preferred, serve the hot smoked BBQ beef short ribs with extra BBQ sauce on the side.

NOTE:

➢ The thickness of the beef short ribs and the smoker's temperature can affect how long they smoke for. Make sure they get the ideal interior temperature for tenderness by using a meat thermometer.

➢ To customize the level of spiciness to your taste, you can change the amount of cayenne pepper in the dry rub.

➢ These short ribs of smoked BBQ beef are ideal for a special occasion or backyard cookout. Savor the succulent, smokey flavor and succulent, fall-off-the-bone flesh!

76. BBQ JACKFRUIT STUFFED SWEET POTATOES

INGREDIENTS:

- ❖ 2 large sweet potatoes
- ❖ 1 can (20 oz) young green jackfruit in brine or water, drained and rinsed
- ❖ 1/2 cup BBQ sauce
- ❖ 1 tablespoon olive oil
- ❖ 1/2 onion, diced
- ❖ 2 cloves garlic, minced
- ❖ Salt and pepper to taste
- ❖ Optional toppings: chopped green onions, chopped cilantro, vegan sour cream

INSTRUCTIONS:

1. Oven preheated at 400°F (200°C).
2. Sweet potatoes should be forked several times after cleaning. Transfer pieces to parchment-lined baking tray.
3. Sweet potatoes should be fork-tender after 45–60 minutes in a heated oven.
4. Bake BBQ jackfruit filling with sweet potatoes. Jackfruit slices can be forked or finger-shredded into pulled pork.
5. Cook olive oil in a skillet over medium heat. Sauté diced onion and minced garlic for 3–4 minutes until fragrant and softened.
6. Put shredded jackfruit, garlic, and onions in the pan. Stir occasionaly for five more minutes.
7. Mix jackfruit and BBQ sauce in a bowl. Simmer 5–10 minutes to combine flavors. Add salt and pepper to taste.
8. Cool sweet potatoes gently after removing them from the oven before handling.
9. Using a fork, mash each sweet potato in half lengthwise and fluff the insides.
10. Fill each sweet potato half to the brim with the BBQ jackfruit mixture by spooning it in evenly.
11. If preferred, garnish with chopped cilantro, green onions, and, if you'd like, a dollop of vegan sour cream.
12. Enjoy your mouthwatering BBQ Jackfruit Stuffed Sweet Potatoes right away after serving!

NOTE:

- ➢ For this dish, use young green jackfruit in water or brine, not syrup.
- ➢ You can change the amount of BBQ sauce to suit your own tastes.
- ➢ In addition to being delicious, these BBQ Jackfruit Stuffed Sweet Potatoes are also gluten-free and vegan, making them a fantastic choice for a filling and healthy dinner.

77. BBQ CHICKEN FLATBREAD WITH CARAMELIZED ONIONS

INGREDIENTS:

For the flatbread:

- ❖ 1 pre-made pizza dough or flatbread
- ❖ 1 cup cooked and shredded chicken breast
- ❖ 1/2 cup BBQ sauce
- ❖ 1 cup shredded mozzarella cheese
- ❖ 1/4 cup thinly sliced red onion
- ❖ Olive oil for brushing

For the caramelized onions:

- ❖ 2 large onions, thinly sliced
- ❖ 2 tablespoons olive oil
- ❖ 1 tablespoon balsamic vinegar
- ❖ Salt and pepper to taste

INSTRUCTIONS:

1. Preheat oven to flatbread or pizza dough temperature.
2. Medium-low heat two teaspoons olive oil in a pan. Sauté thinly sliced onions for 20–30 minutes, turning occasionally, until soft and golden brown.
3. After caramelizing the onions, add the balsamic vinegar and simmer on low for five minutes. Add salt and pepper to taste. Finish cooking and set aside.
4. Spread flatbread or pizza dough on a parchment-lined baking sheet.
5. Brush olive oil on rolled dough.
6. Put shredded chicken breast in a small bowl with BBQ sauce.
7. Apply BBQ chicken mixture evenly to flatbread.
8. Shredded mozzarella cheese tops grilled chicken perfectly.
9. Sprinkle thinly sliced caramelized red onions over cheese.
10. Bake the pizza dough for the appropriate time in a preheated oven until the flatbread is golden brown and the cheese is melted and bubbling.
11. Wait until the flatbread is completely cold before cutting.
12. Slice BBQ Chicken Flatbread in a hot pan.

NOTE:

➤ You may personalize this flatbread by including extra toppings like fried bacon, jalapeños, or diced bell peppers.

➤ Serve this flatbread with BBQ chicken as a starter, a snack, or even a main course for a full dinner when served with a side salad. Savor the flavorful caramelized onions paired with sweet and spicy BBQ chicken over crunchy flatbread!

INGREDIENTS:

For the Hawaiian BBQ Pork:

- ❖ 2 pounds of pork, preferably butt or shoulder, with any excess fat removed and sliced into
- ❖ 1 cup BBQ sauce
- ❖ 1/2 cup pineapple juice
- ❖ 1/4 cup soy sauce
- ❖ 1/4 cup brown sugar
- ❖ 2 cloves garlic, minced
- ❖ 1 teaspoon ground ginger
- ❖ 1/2 teaspoon black pepper
- ❖ Slider buns or dinner rolls
- ❖ Pineapple slices (fresh or canned), for serving
- ❖ Lettuce leaves for serving

INSTRUCTIONS:

1. Mix the BBQ sauce, pineapple juice, soy sauce, brown sugar, ground ginger, minced garlic, and black pepper in a bowl to form the marinade.
2. Spoon the pork bits into a shallow dish or a big resealable plastic bag. Make sure the pork is evenly covered with the marinade as you pour it over it. For optimal flavor, refrigerate the dish or the bag for at least four hours, or overnight.
3. Start the oven at 325°F (163°C).
4. A roasting pan or baking dish should hold the meat and marinade. With the oven preheated, roast the pig wrapped in foil for three to four hours or until tender when poked with a fork.
5. Take the pork out of the oven and use two forks to shred it. In the baking dish, combine the leftover sauce with the shreds of pork.
6. Slicing the dinner rolls or slider buns in half horizontally is how you assemble the sliders. On the bottom half of each sandwich, place a leaf of lettuce and then a dollop of the Hawaiian BBQ pork.
7. After placing a slice of pineapple on top of each slider, cover it with the top half of the bun.
8. Enjoy the Hawaiian Barbecued Pork Sliders right away!

Optional:

➢ For extra flavor, you can optionally cook the pork on a barbecue. Cook it until it's pliable and shirable.

- ➤ You can top with caramelized or grilled onions for an added burst of sweetness and sharpness.
- ➤ These sliders are ideal for potlucks, parties, and game day get-togethers. Family and friends are sure to love these!

79. BBQ CHICKEN LETTUCE WRAPS

INGREDIENTS:

For the BBQ Chicken:

- ❖ one lb boneless, skinless chicken breasts, diced into small pieces
- ❖ 1/2 cup BBQ sauce
- ❖ 1 tablespoon olive oil
- ❖ 1 teaspoon smoked paprika
- ❖ 1/2 teaspoon garlic powder
- ❖ Salt and pepper to taste
- ❖ For the Lettuce Wraps:
- ❖ Large lettuce leaves (such as iceberg, butter, or romaine)
- ❖ 1/2 cup diced tomatoes
- ❖ 1/2 cup diced red onion
- ❖ 1/2 cup diced avocado
- ❖ 1/4 cup chopped fresh cilantro
- ❖ 1/4 cup shredded cheddar cheese (optional)

❖ Lime wedges for serving

INSTRUCTIONS:

1. Mix smoked paprika, olive oil, garlic powder, BBQ sauce, salt, and pepper. Toss the diced chicken in the basin to coat evenly. The suggested fridge marinating time for chicken is 15–60 minutes.
2. Over medium-high heat, preheat a large skillet. When the chicken is marinated and no longer pink, add it to the skillet and cook, tossing now and again for 6 to 8 minutes.
3. After cooking, take the chicken out of the skillet and reserve it.
4. The lettuce leaves should be cleaned, dried, and arranged on a serving tray.
5. Spoon each leaf of lettuce with a little bit of the grilled BBQ chicken.
6. Add diced avocado, diced tomatoes, diced red onion, chopped cilantro, and, if desired, shredded cheddar cheese on top of the chicken.
7. Just before serving, drizzle each lettuce wrap with freshly squeezed lime juice.
8. Enjoy the delicious BBQ Chicken Lettuce Wraps right away!

Optional:

➢ You can add your preferred toppings to these lettuce wraps, like sliced jalapeños, black beans, diced bell peppers, or corn kernels.
➢ Before serving, scatter some smashed tortilla chips over the top of the lettuce wraps for some extra crunch.

➤ A tasty and light dish that's ideal for lunch or dinner are these BBQ Chicken Lettuce Wraps. Since visitors may personalize their wraps with their own toppings, they're also a fantastic entertaining option.

80. SMOKED BBQ CHICKEN WINGS

INGREDIENTS:

- ❖ 2 lbs chicken wings
- ❖ 1/4 cup BBQ rub (store-bought or homemade)
- ❖ 1 cup BBQ sauce (store-bought or homemade)
- ❖ Wood chips or chunks for smoking (hickory, applewood, or cherry work well)

INSTRUCTIONS:

1. Warm up your smoker to 225°F, or 107°C. To use wood chips or chunks in a charcoal smoker, prepare your charcoal and soak it in water for half an hour.
2. Use paper towels to pat dry after rinsing the chicken wings in cold water.
3. After the chicken wings are thoroughly coated, throw them in a big bowl with the BBQ rub.

4. Chicken wings should be placed directly on the smoker racks when the smoker has heated up and started to smoke, with some space between them to allow for airflow.
5. After two or three hours of smoking, the wings should be 165°F (74°C) and have crispy, golden brown skin. Seal the smoker cover.
6. Add plenty of BBQ sauce to the chicken wings and coat them generously on both sides during the final half-hour of smoking.
7. The chicken wings should be taken out of the smoker and placed on a serving tray when they have finished smoking and glazing with BBQ sauce.
8. Warm up some more BBQ sauce for dipping alongside the smoked BBQ chicken wings.

Optional

➤ Add a small metal pan with water or apple juice to the smoker while the chicken wings are smoking if you want to add even more smoke flavor.
➤ To suit your own tastes, feel free to alter the BBQ rub and sauce. Sweetness, spiciness, and tanginess can all be adjusted to your personal preference.
➤ Your next BBQ or game day get-together would be great with these smoked BBQ chicken wings as an appetizer, snack, or main course. Savor the juicy, delicate meat with a delightful smokey flavor!

81. BBQ PULLED PORK GRILLED CHEESE

INGREDIENTS:

- ❖ 8 slices of bread (your choice, but a sturdy bread like sourdough works well)
- ❖ 2 cups BBQ pulled pork (homemade or store-bought)
- ❖ 2 cups shredded cheddar cheese
- ❖ 1/2 cup sliced red onion (optional)
- ❖ Butter, softened, for spreading

INSTRUCTIONS:

1. Heat a griddle or skillet to a medium temperature.
2. Lightly coat one side of every bread piece with melted butter.
3. Put a piece of bread on the skillet with the butter side down. Add shredded cheddar cheese, pulled pork from the barbecue, chopped red onion (if using), and then add extra shredded cheddar cheese on top. Place another piece of bread, butter side up, on top.
4. Cook the sandwich for three to four minutes on each side or until the cheese has melted and the bread is crispy and golden brown.
5. To create more sandwiches, repeat with the remaining bread slices and filling ingredients.
6. After cooking, take the sandwiches out of the skillet and allow them to cool somewhat before slicing.
7. When serving hot, cut each sandwich in half diagonally.

Optional:

➢ You can add pickles, avocado, or sliced jalapeños to personalize your BBQ Pulled Pork Grilled Cheese.
➢ For a full supper, serve the grilled cheese sandwiches with potato chips, a simple green salad, or a side of coleslaw.
➢ These sandwiches are great as a satisfying snack or for lunch or dinner. Savor the savory BBQ pulled pork and oozy cheese sandwiched between buttery, crispy bread slices!

82. BBQ CHICKEN AND RICE CASSEROLE

INGREDIENTS:

- ❖ 2 cups cooked chicken breast and shredded or diced
- ❖ 2 cups cooked rice (white or brown)
- ❖ 1 cup BBQ sauce
- ❖ a half cup of bell pepper, sliced (any color)
- ❖ 1/2 cup of onion, diced
- ❖ 1 cup shredded cheddar cheese
- ❖ 1/4 cup chopped fresh parsley (optional)
- ❖ Salt and pepper to taste
- ❖ Butter or cooking spray for casserole dish

1. Turn the oven on to 350°F, which is 175°C. A 9-by-13-inch baking dish should be greased or sprayed.
2. In a big bowl, combine the cooked chicken breast, basmati rice, barbeque sauce, diced onion, bell pepper, cheddar cheese, chopped fresh parsley (if preferred), salt, and pepper. Mix all the ingredients together.
3. Spread the ingredients out evenly in a baking dish.
4. Reheating the cheese is as easy as roasting the dish with the foil on for 25 to 30 minutes.
5. Bake for 5-10 minutes after removing the foil if you want a browned top.
6. When the dish has cooled for a few minutes, slice it.
7. While the BBQ Chicken and Rice Casserole is cooking, top it with some finely chopped parsley.

Optional Additions:

➢ You may personalize your casserole by adding other ingredients like cooked bacon, sliced tomatoes, corn kernels, or black beans.
➢ For extra crunch, you can also sprinkle breadcrumbs or crumbled tortilla chips on top of the dish.
➢ For a well-balanced supper, serve the casserole with steamed vegetables or a fresh green salad.
➢ Savour this tasty and delightful Rice Casserole with BBQ Chicken for a filling supper that the whole family will love!

84. GRILLED BBQ CHICKEN CAESAR SALAD

INGREDIENTS:

For the Grilled BBQ Chicken:

- ❖ 2 boneless, skinless chicken breasts
- ❖ Salt and pepper to taste
- ❖ 1 cup BBQ sauce
- ❖ 2 tablespoons olive oil

For the Caesar Salad:

- ❖ One huge head of chopped and cleaned romaine lettuce
- ❖ A half cup of Caesar dressing, either made from scratch or purchased
- ❖ 1/4 cup grated Parmesan cheese
- ❖ 1 cup croutons
- ❖ Optional: additional toppings such as cherry tomatoes, sliced cucumber, or avocado.

INSTRUCTIONS:

1. Turn the grill to medium-high heat.
2. Before cooking the chicken breasts, season them with pepper and salt.
3. Combine the olive oil and BBQ sauce in a small bowl. Evenly coat the chicken breasts by brushing them with the mixture.
4. The chicken breasts should be cooked through and have lovely grill marks after placing them on the prepared grill and cooking them for around 6-7 minutes on each side. Ensure that the temperature inside reaches 165°F, or 74°C.
5. Make the Caesar salad while the chicken is roasting. Toss the chopped romaine lettuce with the Caesar dressing in a big bowl until it's well-covered.
6. Arrange the prepared lettuce on individual serving dishes.
7. Allow the chicken to cool for a few minutes after grilling, then thinly slice it.
8. Arrange the Caesar salad with the sliced BBQ chicken on top.
9. Over the chicken, grate some Parmesan cheese.
10. Place croutons over the salad.
11. Add extra toppings, such as avocado, sliced cucumber, or cherry tomatoes, if you'd like.
12. Enjoy the Grilled BBQ Chicken Caesar Salad right away after serving!

Optional:

- ➤ Grilled shrimp or sliced hard-boiled eggs are great protein additions to salads.
- ➤ You may personalize this salad by adding grilled corn, black beans, sliced bell peppers, or anything else you desire.
- ➤ Add some garlicky or crusty bread to the salad for a complete dinner.

85. BBQ BACON WRAPPED MEATLOAF

INGREDIENTS:

For the Meatloaf:

- ❖ 1 lb ground beef
- ❖ 1/2 lb ground pork
- ❖ 1 onion, finely chopped
- ❖ 2 cloves garlic, minced
- ❖ 1/2 cup breadcrumbs
- ❖ 1/4 cup milk
- ❖ 1/4 cup BBQ sauce
- ❖ 1 egg
- ❖ 1 teaspoon Worcestershire sauce
- ❖ 1 teaspoon dried thyme
- ❖ 1 teaspoon dried oregano
- ❖ Salt and pepper to taste

For the Bacon Wrap:

- ❖ 8-10 slices bacon
- ❖ 1/2 cup BBQ sauce (for glazing)

INSTRUCTIONS:

1. Bake at 190^'C (375^'F). Add a wire rack to foil-lined baking sheet.
2. Ground pork, beef, finely chopped garlic and onion, breadcrumbs, milk, Worcestershire sauce, BBQ sauce, egg, dried thyme, dried oregano, salt, and pepper can be mixed in a big basin Mix all ingredients.
3. Form the meat mixture into a loaf on the wire rack.
4. Overlap bacon bits on meatloaf.
5. BBQ sauce evenly on bacon-wrapped meatloaf with pastry brush.
6. Cook bacon in a preheated oven for a few minutes. After reaching 160°F (71°C)
7. , bake the meatloaf for 45–55 minutes.
8. Remove the meatloaf from the oven when it is done cooking and set it aside to rest for a few minutes before slicing.
9. Thickly slice the hot BBQ bacon-wrapped meatloaf and serve it hot.

Optional:

- ➤ You can add chopped herbs, shredded cheese, or diced bell peppers to the meatloaf mixture to make it your own.

- ➢ For a full supper, serve the meatloaf with mashed potatoes, your favorite vegetables, and extra BBQ sauce on the side for dipping.
- ➢ Slices of leftover meatloaf can be kept in the fridge for up to three days if they are kept in an airtight container. They freeze well as well for extended storage.

86. BBQ PORK SPRING ROLLS

INGREDIENTS:

For the BBQ Pork:

- ❖ 1 lb pork tenderloin or pork shoulder, thinly sliced
- ❖ 1/2 cup BBQ sauce
- ❖ 2 tablespoons soy sauce
- ❖ 2 cloves garlic, minced
- ❖ 1 tablespoon brown sugar
- ❖ 1 tablespoon vegetable oil

For the Spring Rolls:

- ❖ 8-10 spring roll rice paper wrappers
- ❖ 2 cups cooked rice vermicelli noodles

- ❖ 1 cup shredded lettuce
- ❖ 1 cup shredded carrots
- ❖ 1 cup thinly sliced cucumber
- ❖ 1/2 cup fresh cilantro leaves
- ❖ 1/4 cup chopped green onions
- ❖ For dipping, hoisin sauce and sweet chili sauce

INSTRUCTIONS:

1. To prepare the BBQ pork, whisk together the brown sugar, soy sauce, minced garlic, and BBQ sauce in a basin.
2. Once the pork pieces are in the marinade, make sure they are thoroughly coated. For optimal flavor, let it marinade in the refrigerator for at least 30 minutes or overnight.
3. In a pan, warm the vegetable oil over medium-high heat. After adding the pork slices, sauté them for 4–5 minutes on each side, or until they are browned and cooked through. After turning off the heat source, store it.

Put the Spring Rolls Together:

1. Get a big bowl or shallow dish ready and fill it with warm water. One rice paper wrapper should be dipped into the heated water for ten to fifteen seconds, or until it becomes malleable and soft.
2. Transfer the softened rice paper wrapper to a sanitized surface, like a moist kitchen towel or chopping board.
3. In the center of the rice paper wrapper, arrange a small amount of cooked rice vermicelli noodles, chopped green onions, shredded lettuce, shredded carrots, sliced cucumber, fresh cilantro leaves, and a few pieces of cooked BBQ pork.

4. After folding the bottom edge up and folding the edges of the rice paper wrapper over the filling, tightly roll the spring roll until it seals. Utilize the remaining parts going forward.

Serve:

➤ Present the BBQ Pork Spring Rolls promptly, along by your preferred dipping sauce, sweet chili sauce, or hoisin sauce.

➤ Optional: Depending on your tastes, you can also add additional ingredients to the spring rolls, like chopped bell peppers, avocado, or mint leaves.

➤ If the spring rolls are made ahead of time, keep them chilled in an airtight container; make sure to cover each one individually with plastic wrap to keep it from sticking. Although they can be kept for up to 24 hours, fresh is when they taste finest.

➤ These BBQ Pork Spring Rolls are ideal for any occasion as a light lunch or refreshing appetizer!

Savor the combination of crispy, fresh veggies and succulent BBQ pork, all encased in delicate rice paper.

87. BBQ CHICKEN STUFFED BELL PEPPERS

INGREDIENT:

- ❖ Cut four large bell peppers (any color) in half and remove the seeds.
- ❖ 2 cups cooked and shredded chicken breast
- ❖ 1 cup cooked quinoa or rice
- ❖ 1/2 cup BBQ sauce (choose your favorite flavor)
- ❖ 1/2 cup diced onion
- ❖ Cut the tops off of half a cup of sliced bell pepper
- ❖ Half a cup of corn kernels, either fresh, frozen, or from a can
- ❖ Half a cup of black beans, drained and rinsed
- ❖ Half a cup of cheddar cheese or shredded Mexican blend cheese
- ❖ 2 tablespoons chopped fresh cilantro (optional)
- ❖ Salt and pepper to taste

❖ Olive oil, for drizzling

INSTRUCTIONS:

1. Either preheat your oven to 375°F (190°C) or your grill to medium heat.
2. The cooked quinoa or rice, shredded chicken, BBQ sauce, corn kernels, black beans, diced onion, diced bell pepper, shredded cheese, chopped cilantro (if using), salt, and pepper should all be appropriately blended in a big dish.
3. Halve the bell peppers and arrange cut side up on a baking sheet or grill-safe dish.
4. Gently push down to stuff the BBQ chicken mixture into each half of a bell pepper.
5. Put the filled bell peppers straight onto the grill grates if you're using one. If you intend to bake the dish in the oven, cover it with aluminum foil.
6. For about 20 to 25 minutes, or until the peppers are soft and the mixture is thoroughly heated, grill or bake the stuffed bell peppers.
7. If you're using a grill, you may cover it as it cooks to let the cheese melt and the peppers cook through.
8. When cooked, take the stuffed bell peppers out of the oven or grill and allow them to cool down before serving.
9. If preferred, garnish with more finely chopped cilantro and serve hot.

NOTE:

➢ You can alter the filling by using additional ingredients such as cooked bacon, chopped spinach, or diced tomatoes.

➢ Although these stuffed bell peppers are a satisfying meal on their own, you can also serve them with grilled vegetables or a side salad for a heartier evening choice.

88. BBQ CHICKEN COBB PIZZA

INGREDIENTS:

For the pizza dough:

- ❖ 1 pound (about 4 cups) pizza dough, store-bought or homemade
- ❖ Cornmeal or flour, for dusting

For the toppings:

- ❖ 1/2 cup BBQ sauce
- ❖ 2 cups cooked and shredded chicken breast
- ❖ 1 cup shredded mozzarella cheese
- ❖ 1/2 cup crumbled blue cheese
- ❖ 1/2 cup diced tomatoes
- ❖ 1/4 cup diced red onion
- ❖ 1/4 cup cooked and crumbled bacon
- ❖ 1/4 cup sliced black olives (optional)
- ❖ 2 tablespoons chopped fresh cilantro (optional)
- ❖ Salt and pepper to taste

INSTRUCTIONS:

1. As stated by your pizza dough, preheat oven to 475°F (245°C). During stove heating, place a pizza stone or baking sheet.
2. Roll pizza dough to your desired thickness on a floured surface. Cornmeal the pizza peel or pan underneath to prevent pizza stones from adhering.
3. Leaving a small boundary for the crust around the borders, evenly spread the BBQ sauce over the pizza dough.
4. Over the BBQ sauce, scatter the mozzarella cheese shreds.
5. Stir a few teaspoons of BBQ sauce into a bowl to coat shredded chicken breast.
6. BBQ chicken should cover the pizza evenly.
7. Top the pizza with cooked and crumbled bacon, blue cheese, tomatoes, red onion, and black olives, if desired.
8. Add salt and pepper to taste.
9. Carefully put the prepared pizza to the pizza stone or baking sheet after preheating the oven.
10. Pizza should be baked for 12–15 minutes until the dough is golden brown and the cheese is melted and bubbling.
11. Let the pizza cool briefly after removing it from the oven.
12. Add finely chopped fresh cilantro for zing.
13. Slice and serve hot pizza.

NOTE:

➤ Change the toppings to your liking. Change parts to suit your tastes.

➤ If your crust-rolling process differs from mine, roll the dough thinner.

➤ This pizza pairs wonderfully with a fresh green salad and tangy vinaigrette.

INGREDIENTS:

For the BBQ Chicken:

- ❖ 2 boneless, skinless chicken breasts
- ❖ 1/2 cup BBQ sauce
- ❖ 1 tablespoon olive oil
- ❖ Salt and pepper to taste

For the Tostadas:

- ❖ 4 tostada shells
- ❖ 1 cup shredded lettuce
- ❖ 1 cup diced tomatoes
- ❖ 1/2 cup diced red onion
- ❖ 1/2 cup rinsed, drained black beans
- ❖ 1/2 cup shredded cheddar

- ❖ 1/4 cup chopped fresh cilantro
- ❖ Lime wedges, for serving (optional)
- ❖ As a garnish, you might choose sour cream or Greek yogurt.
- ❖ Additional BBQ sauce for drizzling (optional)

INSTRUCTIONS:

1. Heat the grill medium-high.
2. Mix olive oil, BBQ sauce, salt, and pepper in a bowl. Toss the chicken breasts in the basin to coat.
3. Before the chicken breasts are no longer pink in the center, grill them for 6 to 8 minutes on each side. The thickness of the chicken breasts determines the cooking time. Add some flavor to fried chicken by slathering it with leftover BBQ sauce.
4. After the chicken is done, take it from the grill and give it a few minutes to rest before slicing or shredding it.
5. Put a tostada shell on a platter and assemble the tostadas. Arrange a layer of black beans, grilled BBQ chicken, chopped tomatoes, diced red onion, and shredded lettuce on top of each shell.
6. Every tostada should have shredded cheddar cheese on top of it.
7. If preferred, garnish with freshly chopped cilantro and a squeeze of lime juice.
8. Serve the grilled BBQ chicken tostadas with Greek yogurt or sour cream, lime wedges, and extra BBQ sauce on the side, if you'd like.

9. Savor your mouthwatering tostadas with grilled BBQ chicken!

NOTE:

- ➢ You can alter the toppings to fit your own tastes. For added taste and texture, add diced bell peppers, sliced jalapeños, or avocado slices.
- ➢ You may make these tasty tostadas with crisp tortillas or even tortilla chips if you don't have tostada shells.
- ➢ These tostadas are ideal for a summer BBQ or other informal get-together as an appetizer or main dish.

90. BBQ BACON WRAPPED POTATO WEDGES

INGREDIENTS:

- ❖ Cut four medium-sized russet potatoes into wedges after cleaning and
- ❖ 8 slices of bacon, cut in half
- ❖ 1/4 cup BBQ sauce
- ❖ 2 tablespoons olive oil
- ❖ 1 teaspoon smoked paprika
- ❖ 1/2 teaspoon garlic powder
- ❖ Salt and black pepper to taste
- ❖ Chopped fresh parsley for garnish (optional)

INSTRUCTIONS:

1. Preheat oven to 400°F (200°C). Prepare a baking pan with parchment or aluminum foil for ease cleanup.
2. In a large bowl, carefully coat the potato wedges with olive oil, smoked paprika, garlic powder, salt, and black pepper.
3. If necessary, use toothpicks to fasten half slices of bacon around each potato wedge. Arrange the potato wedges, covered, on the baking sheet that has been heated and ready.
4. Preheat a baking sheet and bake the potato wedges
5. for 30–35 minutes, tossing them midway through, or until bacon is crisp and potatoes are soft.
6. After taking the baking sheet out of the oven, brush a little BBQ sauce over each potato wedge that has been wrapped in bacon.
7. To achieve caramelized barbecue sauce and golden brown potato wedges, put the baking sheet back in the oven and bake for five to ten more minutes.
8. The potato wedges
9. wrapped in bacon should be taken out of the oven and left to cool for a while after cooking.
10. Warm it up and garnish it with some freshly chopped parsley if you like. It makes a great appetizer or side dish.
11. Savor these delicious potato wedges topped with BBQ bacon!

NOTE:

➤ You can alter this recipe by using your preferred barbecue sauce or by adding more ingredients for taste, including cayenne pepper, onion powder, or chili powder.

➤ To keep wooden toothpicks from burning in the oven, make sure to soak them in water for about half an hour before using.

➤ These BBQ bacon-wrapped potato wedges make a great snack at any time of day or to serve during gatherings and game days.

INGREDIENTS:

- ❖ 16 large white button mushrooms, stems removed and cleaned
- ❖ 1 cup cooked and shredded chicken breast
- ❖ 1/2 cup BBQ sauce
- ❖ 1/4 cup chopped red onion
- ❖ 1/4 cup sliced bell pepper (any color)
- ❖ 1/4 cup shredded mozzarella
- ❖ 2 tablespoons chopped fresh cilantro (optional)
- ❖ Salt and pepper to taste
- ❖ Olive oil, for drizzling

INSTRUCTIONS:

1. Preheat oven to 190°C (375°F). Easy cleanup with aluminum foil or parchment paper on a baking pan.
2. Mix BBQ sauce and chicken breast shreds in a bowl. Mix well.
3. Cap side down, arrange the cleaned mushrooms on the baking sheet that has been prepared.
4. Evenly fill each mushroom cap with the BBQ chicken mixture, gently pressing to cram it in.
5. Top each stuffed mushroom with a sprinkle of diced bell pepper and red onion.
6. Add pepper and salt according to taste.
7. Drizzle the packed mushrooms with shredded mozzarella cheese.
8. To help the stuffed mushrooms brown and crisp up in the oven, drizzle a little olive oil over the top of each one.
9. To achieve soft packed mushrooms and bubbling, melted cheese, bake the mushrooms in a preheated oven for 20 to 25 minutes.
10. Once cooked, remove stuffed mushrooms from oven and set aside to cool.
11. If desired, garnish before serving with finely chopped fresh cilantro.
12. Serve the filled mushrooms with BBQ chicken as a delicious starter or as a part of a larger dinner.

NOTE:

- ➢ By including ingredients like as chopped spinach, cooked bacon, or diced tomatoes
- ➢ , the filling can be enhanced in flavor and texture.
- ➢ These tasty, anytime-of-the-day, BBQ chicken stuffed mushrooms are ideal for gatherings and potlucks.

92. SMOKED BBQ PORK TENDERLOIN

INGREDIENTS:

- ❖ 2 pork tenderloins, each weighing around 1 to 1.5 pounds
- ❖ 1/2 cup BBQ rub or seasoning (store-bought or homemade)
- ❖ 1 cup BBQ sauce (your favorite flavor)
- ❖ Apple wood chips or your preferred smoking wood

INSTRUCTIONS:

1. Set your smoker to 110°C, or 225°F. Light the charcoal in a charcoal smoker and let it get to a steady temperature. Pre-heat a gas smoker in accordance with the manufacturer's recommendations.

2. Trim the pork tenderloins of any excess fat or silver skin while the smoker is heating up. Using paper towels, pat dry the areas.

3. Coat all sides of the pork tenderloins evenly and liberally with the BBQ rub or seasoning. To make sure the seasoning sticks, firmly press it into the flesh.

4. Wood chips need 30 minutes of soaking before usage. Be careful to press out any water.

5. When the smoker is heated, add drained wood chips or coals to smoke.

6. Airflow should be allowed between seasoned pork tenderloins on the smoking rack.

7. For medium-rare pork tenderloin, smoke it with the lid closed at 225°F (110°C) for 1.5 to 2 hours with an internal meat thermometer in the thickest part.

8. While the pork tenderloins are in the last fifteen to twenty minutes of smoking, generously slather them with BBQ sauce on both sides. A tasty coating will be applied to the exterior of the meat by doing this.

9. Once the pork tenderloins have reached the desired internal temperature and are well-glazed, remove them from the smoker and set them on a cutting board.

10. Tent the pork tenderloins loosely with aluminum foil and set aside for five to ten minutes to enable the juices to redistribute.

11. Slice the pork tenderloins into 1/2-inch thick pieces when they have rested. Serve them hot, smothering each slice with any remaining BBQ sauce from the cutting board.

12. Savor the succulent smoked BBQ pork tenderloin together with your preferred sides, including grilled veggies, coleslaw, or baked beans.

NOTE:

> Before smoking the pork tenderloins, inject them with marinade or barbecue sauce using a meat injector to give even more flavor.
> To maintain a constant heat level during the cooking process, keep an eye on the smoker's temperature.
> For up to three to four days, leftover smoked BBQ pork tenderloin can be kept in the refrigerator in an airtight container. It works well with tacos, salads, and sandwiches.

93. BBQ CHICKEN AND CORN SALAD

INGREDIENTS:

For the BBQ Chicken:

- ❖ 2 boneless, skinless chicken breasts
- ❖ 1/2 cup BBQ sauce
- ❖ Salt and pepper to taste
- ❖ Olive oil for grilling

For the Salad:

- ❖ 2 ears of corn, husked
- ❖ Salad greens (e.g., romaine, spinach, arugula)—6 cups
- ❖ 1 cup cherry tomatoes, halved
- ❖ 1/2 red onion, thinly sliced
- ❖ 1 avocado, diced
- ❖ 1/4 cup fresh cilantro, chopped
- ❖ 1/4 cup crumbled feta cheese (optional)

For the Dressing:

- ❖ 1/4 cup BBQ sauce
- ❖ 2 tablespoons olive oil
- ❖ 2 tablespoons apple cider vinegar
- ❖ 1 tablespoon honey
- ❖ 1 teaspoon Dijon mustard
- ❖ Salt and pepper to taste

INSTRUCTIONS:

1. Set your grill's temperature to medium-high.
2. Grill the chicken breasts until they are golden brown and well-seasoned. Lightly coat them with olive oil.
3. The chicken breasts should be cooked through and no longer pink in the center after 6 to 8 minutes on each side of the grill. Brush the chicken breasts with BBQ sauce during the final few minutes of cooking, turning them from time to time to ensure even coating. After cooking, take the chicken from the grill and give it some time to rest before slicing.
4. Season the corn ears with salt and pepper and drizzle with olive oil while the chicken is grilling. Grill, stirring occasionally, until the corn is browned and cooked through, 8 to 10 minutes. Take it off the grill and let it to cool down a bit before slicing the kernels from the cob.
5. Mix the mixed salad greens, grilled corn kernels, diced avocado, sliced red onion, chopped cilantro, and cherry tomatoes in a big salad dish.

6. To prepare the dressing, combine the BBQ sauce, olive oil, Dijon mustard, honey, apple cider vinegar, salt, and pepper in a small bowl.
7. Thinly slice the chicken breasts that have been grilled.
8. To the salad dish, add the cut chicken.
9. Pour the salad dressing over everything and gently toss to coat everything equally.
10. If preferred, garnish the salad with some crumbled feta cheese.
11. Enjoy the delicious BBQ chicken and corn salad right away!

NOTE:

➢ For added taste and texture, feel free to modify the salad by adding extras like grilled pineapple, sliced bell peppers, or black beans.

➢ It is possible to make the salad dressing in advance and refrigerate it until it is needed. Before tossing it with the salad, give it a good shake or stir.

➢ This recipe for barbecued chicken and corn salad is ideal for any time of year as a light and refreshing supper or as part of a potluck during the summer.

94. GRILLED BBQ CHICKEN AND VEGGIE FOIL PACKETS

INGREDIENTS:

- ❖ Two chicken breasts that have been removed the skin and bones and chopped into little pieces
- ❖ 1 cup BBQ sauce
- ❖ 2 large bell peppers, sliced
- ❖ 1 large red onion, sliced
- ❖ 2 medium zucchini, sliced
- ❖ 2 medium yellow squash, sliced
- ❖ 8-10 cherry tomatoes
- ❖ 2 tablespoons olive oil
- ❖ Toss with salt and pepper.
- ❖ Garnish with chopped fresh herbs (such basil or parsley, if desired).

INSTRUCTIONS:

1. Set your grill's temperature to medium-high.
2. Coat the chicken pieces in BBQ sauce by tossing them in a bowl. Put aside.
3. Tear out four large (12–14 inch long) strips of heavy-duty aluminum foil.
4. Arrange the foil pieces in the center and evenly divide the sliced bell peppers, red onion, zucchini, yellow squash, and cherry tomatoes.
5. Sprinkle salt and pepper over the vegetables after pouring olive oil over them. Toss softly.
6. Top each vegetable mixture with an equal amount of the chicken pieces covered in barbecue sauce.
7. To keep any juices from seeping out while grilling, fold the foil's sides over the chicken and veggies to form a package and close the edges firmly.
8. After preheating the grill, place the foil packets on it and cook for 15 to 20 minutes, or until the chicken is thoroughly cooked and the vegetables are soft. Using tongs, carefully turn the packets halfway through the cooking time.
9. After cooking, carefully open the foil packages to ensure doneness (be cautious around steam). Take the packets from the grill if the chicken and veggies are done to your preference. If not, reseal the packages and cook for a further few minutes on the grill.
10. Gently pour each foil packet's contents into a separate plate or bowl.
11. If preferred, garnish with finely chopped fresh herbs and serve hot.

12. Savor your tasty and easy foil packages of grilled BBQ chicken and veggies!

NOTE:

➢ You can alter the vegetables to suit your tastes or what you happen to have on hand. Feel free to add more vegetables, such as broccoli, asparagus, or mushrooms, or to substitute them.

➢ The foil packets should be handled carefully since they will be hot when you take them out of the grill.

➢ These foil packets provide a filling and substantial dinner when served with crusty bread, quinoa, or rice.

95. BBQ PULLED CHICKEN STUFFED POTATOES

INGREDIENTS:

- ❖ 4 large russet potatoes
- ❖ 2 boneless, skinless chicken breasts
- ❖ 1 cup BBQ sauce
- ❖ 1/2 cup shredded cheddar cheese
- ❖ 1/4 cup sliced green onions
- ❖ 1/4 cup sour cream (optional)
- ❖ Salt and pepper to taste
- ❖ Olive oil for brushing

INSTRUCTIONS:

- ❖ Heat oven to 400°F (200°C).
- ❖ Post-scrubbing, pat potatoes dry with paper towels. Make fork marks on each potato.
- ❖ Toss the potatoes with salt after rubbing them with olive oil. Afterwards, place them on a baking sheet coated with aluminum foil.
- ❖ In order for a fork to come out soft when stuck into the potatoes, bake them for 45 to 60 minutes.
- ❖ Pulled chicken from
- ❖ the BBQ can be made while the potatoes are in the oven. After the chicken breasts have been seasoned, include salt and pepper.
- ❖ High heat is used to grill pans or grills. It should take around 6 to 8 minutes per side on the grill for the chicken breasts to cook all the way through and remove any pinkness from the center.
- ❖ After the chicken is cooked, shred it using two forks.
- ❖ A pot set over medium heat should be used to heat the BBQ sauce. Before you add the shredded chicken to the sauce, m
- ❖ ake sure the chicken is properly coated.
- ❖ Before slicing each roasted potato in half lengthwise, be careful not to cut across.
- ❖ Inspect the potatoes and use a fork to fluff them inside. Spoon out equal portions of the BBQ pulled chicken mixture and divide them among the potatoes.
- ❖ Shredded cheddar cheese is the ideal garnish for any loaded potato.
- ❖ To make sure the cheese melts and bubbles, pop

- ❖ the potatoes back into the oven for 5 to 10 minutes after stuffing.
- ❖ After the baked potatoes have cooled, top them with chopped green onions.
- ❖ If you'd like, you can top the hot potatoes with sour cream and BBQ pulled chicken.
- ❖ Savor each mouthful of your filling meal!

NOTE:

- ➢ The toppings for these filled potatoes can be changed to suit your tastes. For added taste and texture, try adding chopped cilantro, cubed avocado, or crispy bacon.
- ➢ Refrigerate leftover BBQ pulled chicken for up to three to four days in an airtight container. It works well for preparing salads, wraps, and sandwiches.

96. BBQ CHICKEN AND PINEAPPLE PIZZA

INGREDIENTS:

For the Pizza Dough:

- ❖ 1 pound pizza dough, store-bought or homemade
- ❖ Cornmeal or flour, for dusting

For the Toppings:

- ❖ 1/2 cup BBQ sauce
- ❖ 1 cup cooked and shredded chicken breast
- ❖ 1 cup pineapple chunks, fresh or canned
- ❖ 1/2 cup sliced red onion
- ❖ 1 cup shredded mozzarella cheese
- ❖ 1/4 cup chopped fresh cilantro
- ❖ Crushed red pepper flakes (optional)
- ❖ Olive oil, for drizzling

INSTRUCTIONS:

1. Set the oven's temperature to its maximum setting (often 500°F or 260°C). If you plan to use a pizza stone, warm that in the oven as well.
2. Preheat a floured surface and roll out pizza dough to the thickness you like. If you're using a pizza stone, sprinkle cornmeal over the peel or baking sheet to keep the pizza from sticking.
3. After you've left some room around the pizza dough's edges for the crust, spread BBQ sauce evenly.
4. On top of the barbecue sauce, evenly distribute the shredded chicken.
5. On top of the
6. chicken, toss in some pineapple chunks and chopped red onion.
7. On top of the pizza, crumble some mozzarella.
8. The toppings will brown and crisp up more easily in the oven if you sprinkle a little olive oil over them.
9. If you prefer your pizza on the spicy side, you can top it with crushed red pepper flakes.
10. After the pizza is built, carefully transfer it to the oven-ready baking sheet or pizza stone.
11. Brown the crust and bring the cheese to a boil in about 10 to 12 minutes in the oven.
12. After baking, let the pizza cool.
13. Garnish with some freshly chopped cilantro just before serving.
14. Keep the pizza warm after slicing.
15. Take a bite off of that BBQ chicken and pineapple pizza!

➢ Please feel free to customize the toppings to your liking. Bell peppers, fried bacon, or chopped jalapeños
➢ can be added for more flavor and texture.

97. SMOKED BBQ CHICKEN LEGS

INGREDIENTS:

- ❖ 8 chicken legs
- ❖ 1 cup BBQ sauce (your favorite flavor)
- ❖ 2 tablespoons olive oil
- ❖ 2 tablespoons paprika
- ❖ 1 tablespoon garlic powder
- ❖ 1 tablespoon onion powder
- ❖ 1 tablespoon brown sugar
- ❖ 1 teaspoon salt
- ❖ 1 teaspoon black pepper
- ❖ Optional: additional BBQ rub or seasoning for extra flavor

INSTRUCTIONS:

1. Remove any extra skin or fat from the chicken legs before cooking. Pat the spots dry using paper towels.

2. To make a spice rub, combine the olive oil, paprika, onion and garlic powders, brown sugar, salt, and black pepper in a small bowl.

3. Coat the chicken legs on both sides by equally rubbing them with the spice mixture. For added taste, you can, if you'd like, season or massage the chicken with more BBQ rub.

4. While you set up your smoker, leave the seasoned chicken legs to rest at room temperature.

5. Light your smoker with your favorite smoking wood (hickory, apple, or cherry) and preheat it to 225°F (107°C).

6. After preheating the smoker, put the chicken legs straight onto the grill grates after seasoning.

7. After the chicken legs have reached an internal temperature of 165°F (74°C), take a meat thermometer and place it into the thickest part of the flesh, making sure not to contact the bone. Then, cover the smoker and let the legs smoke for around an hour to two hours.

8. During the last half an hour of smoking, generously coat the chicken legs with BBQ sauce using a brush. To ensure even cooking and a generous coating of BBQ sauce, baste the chicken approximately once every 10 minutes.

9. After the chicken legs have cooked, remove them from the smoker with care and set them on a dish.

10. After resting for a few minutes, the chicken legs will absorb more of the juices.

11. Pair the sizzling smoked BBQ chicken legs with grilled vegetables, coleslaw, or cornbread, as your choice of side dish.
12. Those juicy, smoky chicken legs from the BBQ are calling your name.

NOTE:

- ➤ To ensure a steady heat level during the cooking process, keep an eye on the smoker's temperature.
- ➤ You can use your preferred homemade or store-bought sauce to personalize the BBQ sauce. Try a variety of flavor combinations until you find your favorite.
- ➤ For up to three to four days, leftover smoked BBQ chicken legs can be kept in the refrigerator in an airtight container. They work well for tacos, salads, and sandwiches.

98. BBQ CHICKEN AND CHEDDAR STUFFED PRETZELS

INGREDIENTS:

For the Pretzel Dough:

- ❖ One and a half cups of warm (110–115°F) water
- ❖ 1 packet (2 and 1/4 teaspoons) active dry yeast
- ❖ 1 teaspoon granulated sugar
- ❖ 4 cups all-purpose flour
- ❖ 1 teaspoon salt
- ❖ 1/4 cup baking soda
- ❖ 1 large egg, beaten (for egg wash)
- ❖ Coarse sea salt, for sprinkling
- ❖ For the BBQ Chicken Filling:
- ❖ 1 cup cooked and shredded chicken breast
- ❖ 1/2 cup BBQ sauce
- ❖ 1/2 cup shredded cheddar cheese

- ❖ 2 green onions, finely chopped

INSTRUCTIONS:

1. A small basin should contain yeast, sugar, and warm water. Expect 5-10 minutes of bubbly pleasure.
2. Combine the salt and flour in a large basin or stand mixer. Mix the yeast mixture with the dough.
3. By kneading the dough for five minutes on a floured surface, by hand, or using the dough hook attachment of a stand mixer, achieve a smooth and elastic texture.
4. While the dough rests in a greased, heated basin, drape a clean dishcloth over it. Within an hour, it ought to have doubled.
5. Bake at 425°F (220°C) in a preheated oven. Spread out on a baking tray.
6. Combine the cooked and shredded chicken breast with the BBQ sauce in a small bowl, stirring to coat each piece evenly.
7. After the dough has risen, punch it down and divide it into 8 equal halves.
8. Each dough part should be rolled into an 18-inch-long rope.
9. Roll out each dough rope into an approximately 4-inch-wide rectangle.
10. Leaving a small boundary around the edges, place a spoonful of the BBQ chicken mixture onto each rectangle of dough.
11. Over the BBQ chicken mixture, scatter chopped green onions and grated cheddar cheese.
12. Starting from the long side of the dough, tightly roll it up to enclose the filling and create a log.

13. To seal, press the dough's edges together.
14. Create a loop out of each filled dough log, fold the ends over one another, and press them onto the loop's lower curve to make a pretzel shape.
15. Heat the water in a big pot until it boils. Carefully pour in the baking soda and stir to dissolve (it may bubble up) in the boiling water.
16. One or two pretzels at a time, carefully drop them into the hot water and cook for about 30 seconds on each side. This process will contribute to the pretzels' distinctive golden hue and chewy texture.
17. Using a slotted spoon, remove the boiling pretzels from the water and put them on the baking sheet that has been prepared.
18. Sprinkle coarse sea salt and whip egg over the tops of the pretzels.
19. The pretzels should be baked for 12 to 15 minutes, or until they are cooked through and golden brown.
20. Before serving, take the pretzels out of the oven and allow them to cool somewhat.
21. Warm up with your tasty BBQ chicken and cheddar-stuffed pretzels!

NOTE:

➢ You can alter the filling by using your preferred BBQ sauce or by including extras like caramelized onions, fried bacon, or jalapeños for a kick of flavor.
➢ While leftovers can be kept in an airtight container at room temperature for one to two days, they are best

consumed fresh the day they are cooked. To enjoy them warm and gooey, reheat them in the oven or microwave before serving.

99. BBQ PORK EGG ROLLS

INGREDIENTS:

For the BBQ Pork Filling:

- ❖ One cup of cooked, shredded pork (such leftover pulled pork or BBQ pork)
- ❖ half a cup barbecue sauce
- ❖ one-fourth cup finely chopped onions
- ❖ 1/4 cup bell pepper, chopped
- ❖ 2 cloves garlic, minced
- ❖ 1 tablespoon vegetable oil
- ❖ Salt and pepper to taste

For the Egg Rolls:

- ❖ 12 egg roll wrappers
- ❖ 1 egg, beaten (for sealing the wrappers)

❖ Vegetable oil, for frying

INSTRUCTIONS:

1. Cook vegetable oil in a skillet or frying pan over medium heat. Add minced garlic, onion, and bell pepper. Cook 3–4 minutes until tender.
2. Add the cooked and shredded pork to the skillet along with the BBQ sauce. Cook for a further two to three minutes, stirring frequently, or until well cooked. Season with salt and pepper, to taste. After removing the filling from the burner, allow it to cool a bit.
3. Arrange an egg roll wrapper so that one corner faces you, creating a diamond shape, on a clean surface. About 2 teaspoons of the BBQ pork filling
4. should be centered in the wrapper.
5. Fold the wrapper so that the side corners are tucked in and the bottom corner is over the filling. Tightly roll the wrapper away from you, sealing the upper corner with the
6. beaten egg. Proceed with the leftover filling and the wrappers.
7. One by one, carefully drop a few egg rolls into the heated oil and cook for three to four minutes on each side, or until golden brown and crispy. Halfway through cooking, turn them with tongs.
8. After the egg rolls are crispy and golden brown, remove them from the oil and set them aside to drain on a tray covered with paper towels.
9. Serve the spicy sweet chili sauce, additional BBQ sauce, or your favorite dipping sauce
10. alongside the BBQ pork egg rolls.

11. Enjoy your delicious homemade BBQ pork and egg rolls!

NOTE:

- ➤ If you want to give the combination more crunch and texture, you can add veggies like shredded cabbage, carrots, or water chestnuts.
- ➤ Heat oven to 400°F/200°C. Transfer fried egg rolls to a parchment-lined baking sheet. This replaces egg rolls with frying. Bake them to golden brown and crispy with a light vegetable oil coating for 15–20 minutes.

INGREDIENTS:

For the BBQ Chicken:

- ❖ 2 boneless, skinless chicken breasts
- ❖ 1/2 cup BBQ sauce
- ❖ Salt and pepper to taste
- ❖ Olive oil for grilling

For the Pita Pockets:

- ❖ 4 large pita bread rounds
- ❖ 1 cup shredded lettuce
- ❖ 1 large tomato, diced
- ❖ 1/2 red onion, thinly sliced
- ❖ 1/2 cup shredded cheddar cheese
- ❖ 1/4 cups of freshly chopped parsley or cilantro
- ❖ Optional: sliced avocado, sliced cucumber, sliced bell peppers

INSTRUCTIONS:

1. Heat your grill to medium-high.
2. Season chicken breasts with salt and pepper. Apply a little olive oil.
3. The chicken breasts should be cooked through and no longer pink in the center after 6–8 minutes on each side of the grill. Turn the chicken breasts occasionally to coat them evenly with BBQ sauce in the final minutes of cooking. After grilling, let the chicken rest before slicing.
4. While the chicken cooks until browned and heated through, toast the pita bread rounds for one to two minutes on each side of the grill.
5. Thinly slice grilled chicken breasts.
6. Make pita pockets by halving each pita bread round before assembly.
7. Each pita pocket
8. should have plenty of chopped tomato, red onion, shredded lettuce, and grilled chicken strips.
9. Top each pita pocket
10. with shredded cheddar cheese.
11. Garnish with finely chopped parsley or cilantro.
12. You can pack pita pockets with sliced bell peppers, avocados, or cucumbers for flavor and texture.
13. Eat the grilled BBQ chicken pita pockets immediately!

NOTE:

➢ Adjust toppings to suit your preferences on pita pockets. Add or substitute pickles, olives, or cheese.

➢ These pita pockets with grilled BBQ chicken are perfect for picnics and weeknight dinners.

Barbecue, in all its forms and flavors, is a testament to the universal love of cooking and sharing good food. Whether you are drawn to the smoky depths of American BBQ, the interactive and flavorful Korean BBQ, the festive Brazilian churrasco, or the simple yet exquisite Japanese yakitori, there is something inherently joyous about the barbecue experience.

The Essence of BBQ

At its core, barbecue is about more than just food; it's about connection. It's the laughter shared over a grill, stories about a smoking pit, and the communal joy of a perfectly cooked piece of meat. BBQ is a social activity that brings people together, transcending cultural and geographical boundaries.

Embracing the BBQ Journey

Embarking on your barbecue journey means embracing the tradition and innovation this cooking method offers. It's about experimenting with different meats, spices, and techniques and discovering what makes your taste buds sing. The recipes in this collection are designed to inspire you, whether you're cooking for a casual family dinner or hosting a grand outdoor feast.

Tips for BBQ Success

Preparation is Key: From marinating to setting up your grill, proper preparation is crucial for BBQ success. Take the time to season your meat well and set up your cooking area safely and efficiently.

Patience Pays Off: A great barbecue often requires patience. Low and slow cooking methods, like smoking, allow flavors to develop and meats to become tender. Don't rush the process; enjoy the journey.

Experiment and Have Fun: BBQ is as much about creativity as it is about tradition. Don't be bold; try new marinades, rubs, or even new types of meat. Each experiment is a learning experience that can lead to delicious discoveries.

The Lasting Impact of BBQ

As you delve into the barbecue world, remember that it's more than a cooking technique; it's a way to create lasting memories. Whether it's the smell of hickory smoke wafting through the air, the sound of sizzling meat or the sight of friends and family gathered around; barbecue has a special ability to leave an enduring impression on our palates and emotions.

Final Thoughts

Barbecue is a celebration of flavor, culture, and community. It's a culinary tradition that invites you to slow down, savor each bite, and enjoy the process as much as the outcome. With the recipes and tips in this collection, you are well-equipped to explore the diverse and delightful world of BBQ.

So fire up the grill, let the smoke work its magic, and relish the art of barbecue. Here's to many delicious meals, memorable gatherings, and the joyous spirit of barbecue that brings us all together. Enjoy your barbecue adventures!

THE END

Made in United States
Troutdale, OR
06/03/2024